INDIAN HERITAGE COOKERY

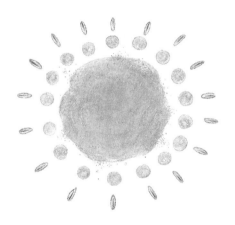

By Julie Sahni

Illustrated by Wayne Anderson

WALKER BOOKS

For Rod
With love and many unspoken words of gratitude and
thanks to Jill Norman for her help and support.

Designer: Jim Bunker

First published 1988 by Walker Books Ltd
87 Vauxhall Walk, London SE11 5HJ

Text © 1988 Julie Sahni
Illustrations © 1988 Walker Books Ltd

Printed and bound in Italy
by L.E.G.O., Vicenza

British Library Cataloguing in Publication Data
Sahni, Julie
Indian heritage cookery.
1. Cookery, Indian
I. Title
641.3'00954   TX724.5.14
ISBN 0-7445-0772-3
ISBN 0-7445-0714-6 Pbk

CONTENTS

INTRODUCTION

Indian cooking, commonly believed to be a bowl of curry, is in fact not one single style of cooking at all. It is an amalgamation of several cuisines representing the varying geographical features of the nation, its cultural heritage and the religious beliefs of its people. The terrain and climate of India are indeed extremely varied. They range from snow-covered Kashmir in the northern Himalayan mountains to the sultry Malabar coast in the deep south, from the lush slopes of Darjeeling in the east to the sprawling Rajasthan desert of the west. India has also been constantly awakened, gastronomically, by the swarm of invading cultures over a period of several centuries. These include Moslems, Portuguese, Persians, French and British. They each introduced new religious beliefs and practices along with new food and cooking concepts.

Hindus are the predominant religious group in India. The Jains, Sikhs and Buddhists, who were all once a part of the Hindu religion, are today distinctly separate groups and form a sizable minority. Together they have laid the foundation of Indian cooking. It is their cuisines in their innumerable interpretations that have come to be known as the regional cooking of India. Of particular importance are two sub-groups: the Hindu Brahmins (one of the four castes of the Hindus) and the Jain. They are both strictly vegetarian and thus eliminate all forms of meat, fish and their by-products from their daily diet. Their religious taboos and dietary restrictions have helped shape India's vegetarian cuisine to an unparalleled sophistication. Also worth mentioning here are those special cultural groups that emerged from foreign influence and whose impact on the regional cuisine has been profound. The *vindaloo* of Goanese Christians (of Portuguese descent), the *dhan-shak* of Parsees (of Persian descent), and the kedgeree, mango fool and roasts of the Anglo-Indians are today world-famous dishes.

The Moslems are the largest minority group in India. They are credited with introducing the exquisite Moghul culture to India that gave the world, among other splendours, the Taj Mahal. It was in the royal courts and kitchens of the Moghuls that the most refined of all regional cuisines was born. This style of cooking, with its traces of Persian and Turkish influence, is typified by creamy mellow sauces, subtle fragrances and exquisite garnishes and is called classic Indian cooking, or more commonly, Moghul cooking.

Thus one sees a beautiful array of food ranging from the cardamom-smothered braised lamb of the Moghuls to the fiery curries of the Goans; the mustard-laced seafoods of the Bengalis to the seductive cinnamon-perfumed roast chicken with plums of the Anglo-Indians. This is Indian food in all its intricacies and complexity. On close examination one sees that Indian food can in fact be identified as a whole. The element that ties all these styles of cooking together is the extensive use of herbs and spices. Indian cooks develop this knowledge with meticulous care and passion from the day they first experience life, thus developing skills unsurpassed in the culinary world.

Finally, the most wonderful aspect of Indian cooking is that complex flavourings are achieved by non-complex cooking techniques. In other words, Indian cooking is uncomplicated, quick and inexpensive. All you need is a desire to awaken your senses with aromas and flavours.

Julie Sahni

— 1 —
THE INDIAN KITCHEN

Indian cooking is known as the most complexly flavoured and the most aromatic of the world's cuisines. This magical sensation is created by herbs and spices, which are the foundation of Indian cooking. They are used not just to flavour food but to give colour, piquancy, hotness and texture to the finished dish. Knowledge of spices and herbs – how they interact with food to bring out the desired flavour – has to be mastered in order to become a natural Indian cook.

If you are concerned with the health aspects of eating spices, there is no need for alarm. Spices and herbs have medicinal properties, and so are good for one's body, mind and soul. They act as preservatives, an added benefit as the dishes can be prepared ahead and refrigerated for several days without any change in flavour or appearance.

Spices are organic matter and must be cooked in order for them to be digested easily. For this reason spices are always put into a dish at the beginning, or at least early, during the cooking. When spices are sprinkled over a finished dish such as a yogurt salad or a drink they must be precooked. This is done by placing the whole spices in a frying pan and toasting until they turn several shades darker and exude a roasted aroma, then they are ground.

Spices should be purchased whole (except for cayenne, ground ginger and turmeric which are sold in powdered form only) and stored in airtight containers in a cool, dry place. Spices release more fragrance when crushed, so they are generally added to dishes in ground form. To grind spices use a spice or coffee mill or a mortar and pestle. Grind only small quantities of spices as needed, as ground spices quickly go stale.

In India herbs are cultivated all year round and always used fresh, never dried. Herbs are chopped and mixed into dishes or used as a garnish. They may be chopped and mixed with fresh ginger root, spices and yogurt to serve as relishes and dips, or brewed with ginger root and honey in herbal teas.

Most spices and herbs used in Indian cooking are widely available. A few of the more unusual, such as tamarind or lovage (carom) can be found in Indian or Pakistani grocery shops but in all cases I have given more readily available alternatives (see the following pages).

Finally, remember, spices and herbs are sensual seasonings. Like perfume, they must be handled with a delicate touch – just enough to tease the palate, leaving behind a trail of exotic intrigue and haunting scents.

Asafoetida (*Heeng*)
This is a strong-smelling spice, available in powdered form. It is used by certain religious groups to give an onion-like flavour to food as they are prohibited to use onions as seasoning. Very logically, a little chopped onion makes an excellent substitute for asafoetida.

Cardamom (*Elaichi*)
These are small ¼ in/5 mm long green or white pods containing highly aromatic round black seeds. Cardamom is used either in whole pod form, as in rice pilafs and braised curries, or in powdered form as in desserts and sauces. In the latter case the pods are peeled, skins discarded and the seeds finely ground to a powder.

Chapati Flour (*Atta*)
Chapati flour, known as *atta* in Hindi, is finely ground whole wheat kernels with the germ and husk intact. It is rich in nutrients and flavour and the dough made with this flour is non-rubbery and thus easy to roll. Stone-ground wholemeal flour makes a good substitute.

Chick-pea or Gram Flour (*Besan*)
Dried chick-peas are ground into a fine flour which is called chick-pea flour or gram flour, or *besan* in Hindi. High in protein, chick-pea flour is preferred in batters for its spicy flavour and for the crackling texture it lends to fritters.

Chilli Powder or Cayenne Pepper (*Lal Mirch*)
This is the red devil's powder that gives food a hot taste. By adding more or less chilli powder, you can regulate the hotness of the dish. Red chilli pods ground to a powder, red Italian pepper flakes or fresh green chillies (p. 15) all make good substitutes.

Cinnamon (*Dalchini*)
We are all familiar with the use of ground cinnamon in baking cakes and pies. In Indian cooking, cinnamon is primarily used in stick form, generally 3 in/7 cm long, in savoury dishes to lend a subtle fragrance to pilafs and meat dishes, and to create spiced tea infusions.

Clove (*Laung*)
Fragrant and pungent, cloves are used both whole and ground in stews, casseroles, pilafs and chutneys. Whole cloves are used where it is important not to tint the colour of the dish, such as in white rice pilaf and fish preparations.

Coconut (*Narial*)
Grated, flaked or in milk form, coconut is an important ingredient in Indian cooking. Grated coconut is used for its texture and visual appeal

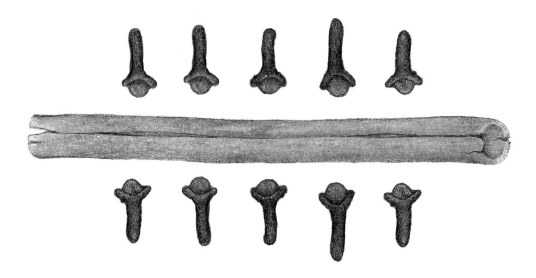

while coconut milk is added to give a sweet rich flavour to the sauce. Coconut milk may be made from a block of creamed coconut, or single or double cream makes an acceptable substitute. Unsweetened desiccated coconut flakes can replace fresh grated coconut. Making fresh grated coconut and coconut milk is in fact very simple.

Grated Coconut: buy a coconut that has no cracks and is heavy with liquid. Pierce the eyes of the coconut with a knife or chisel, drain off the liquid and discard. Place the coconut in a preheated oven, gas 5/375°F/190°C, for 25 minutes. Remove the coconut and whack with a hammer to crack it and release the meat inside. Peel the brown skin off the coconut meat and cut the meat into 1 in/2.5 cm pieces. Grind the coconut in batches in an electric blender or a food processor. An average-sized coconut will yield about 10 oz/300 g grated coconut.

Coconut Milk: to each 3 oz/75 g grated coconut, add 8 fl oz/250 ml boiling water or milk. Soak for 30 minutes and then purée the mixture in batches using a blender or food processor. Strain the liquid through a double layer of muslin, squeezing the pulp as much as possible. An average-sized coconut will yield 1¼ pt/750 ml coconut milk.

Coriander – spice and herb (*Dhania*)

These small peppercorn-like seeds with pungent flavour are the spice that is used in pickling spice mixtures and in pickled cucumbers. Coriander seeds are usually ground and are used in innumerable dishes throughout India. Coriander is used in large quantities in both curry powder (p. 14) and garam masala (p. 14).

Ground roasted coriander seeds are added to finished yogurt salads and cold appetizers to impart a smoky aroma.

To roast, put coriander seeds (2-4 tablespoons) in a small, dry frying pan. Roast the spices over moderately high heat, stirring and turning constantly, until the seeds are several shades darker and exude a spicy aroma (about 5 minutes). Transfer them to a bowl, cool completely, then grind into a fine powder using a spice or coffee mill, or a mortar and pestle.

Coriander leaves are from the same plant as coriander seeds. It is coriander leaves that give dishes the characteristic pungent aroma generally associated with Indian food. It is used just as one uses parsley here. Parsley makes an acceptable substitute (primarily for visual appeal because it lacks the distinctive taste of coriander).

Cumin (*Jeera*)

These tiny greenish-brown seeds, resembling caraway in shape, are the most important spice in Indian cooking, providing another familiar aroma associated with Indian food. Cumin is used both whole and ground.

Ground roasted cumin seeds are sprinkled on finished yogurt and vegetable salads, relishes, drinks and cold appetizers, to give that special smoky-spicy flavour. It is also used in stews and braised meats at the end of cooking to perk up the flavours in the dish. To roast and grind cumin seeds follow the instructions given for roasting and grinding coriander seeds (p. 13).

Curry Powder (*Kari Podi*)

A wonderfully delicious spice blend from southern India, curry powder can create magic if imaginatively used. In Indian cooking it is used in vegetable dishes, stews, soups and sauces. Curry powder is widely available. It is also very easy to make at home. Here is a classic recipe that is mild and fragrant.

Curry Powder: combine 3 tablespoons ground coriander, 1 tablespoon turmeric and 1 teaspoon each of ground cumin, mustard powder, black pepper, chilli powder and ground fenugreek (or dill weed). Store in an airtight jar.

Fennel (*Saunf*)

Fennel seeds, pale green in colour, look like fat caraway seeds. They are ground and used in sauces, sweets and desserts. In Bengal, whole fennel seeds are used for flavouring vegetables and lentils. Fennel is an excellent digestive and mouth refresher frequently chewed by Indians as an after-dinner mint. Fennel and aniseed can be used interchangeably.

Fenugreek (*Methi*)

These tiny brown bitter-tasting beans are an important spice, particularly in the southern regions of India. Known to counteract flatulence, fenugreek is often added to starchy vegetables, dried beans and peas. Dill seeds make a reasonable substitute for fenugreek.

Garam Masala

This is a highly aromatic blend of spices created to lace the Moghul dishes of the royal courts in northern India. It is sprinkled or folded into a finished braised or stewed dish to give it a roasted flavour. Commercial garam masala is available but it can also be made easily at home.

Garam Masala: combine 1 tablespoon each of whole cumin and coriander seeds, 1 teaspoon each

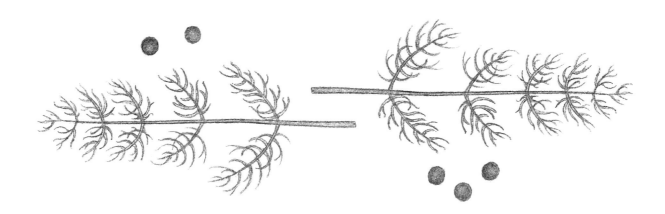

of black peppercorns and cardamom seeds (ground or whole), ½ teaspoon cloves, and a 2 in/5 cm piece cinnamon (broken up), in a frying pan. Roast, following the instructions for roasting coriander seeds (p. 13). Grind the spice mixture to a fine powder and stir in ¼ teaspoon grated nutmeg. Store in an airtight jar.

Ginger – fresh and ground (*Adrak*)
Fresh ginger, the aromatic rhizome used extensively in oriental cooking is also an important flavouring in Indian cooking. It is used as a seasoning for vegetables and lentils, in pilafs and braised meats, and in chutneys and in herbal tea infusions. Ginger is regarded as a digestive, hence it is always added to beans and peas and vegetables high in starch. If fresh ginger is unavailable, dry ginger (1 teaspoon dried for 1 tablespoon fresh ginger) may be substituted.

Ground ginger, as you can guess, is made by powdering sun-dried fresh ginger slices. It is used in kebabs, relishes, chutneys and Kashmiri meat preparations. Although fresh ginger and ground ginger can be used interchangeably, they really aren't similar in taste. Ground ginger is sweet and woody while fresh is spicy and herbal. Therefore try to use fresh ginger whenever possible. Fresh

ginger is always peeled before using.

Green Chilli (*Hari Mirch*)
Green chillies are added to a dish not just for their hotness but also to impart a herbal aroma. In addition, chillies are rich in vitamins A and D. For a milder taste split and deseed chillies before use. If green chillies are unavailable, ¼ teaspoon chilli powder for 1 green chilli makes a good substitute. In recipes calling for several green chillies you may also wish to add a little chopped green pepper for a herbal flavour.

A word of caution: chillies should be handled with care as they cause a burning sensation and irritation when touched. You may like to use rubber or surgical gloves to protect your hands, or prepare them under running water and be sure not to rub your eyes while handling chillies.

Jaggery and Jaggery Syrup (*Gudh*)
Jaggery is unrefined lump cane, or palm, sugar. The concentrated cane syrup, just before it sets and turns into jaggery, is called jaggery syrup. Both are used in Indian cooking to lend a sweet taste and a distinct, maple-like flavour to the dish. Dark and light brown sugar mixed in equal proportions makes an acceptable substitute.

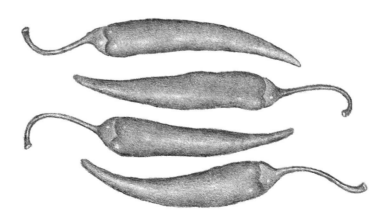

Lovage (*Ajwain*)

Also known as carom, these tiny seeds resemble celery seeds. When slightly crushed they exude a thyme-like aroma. They are used in salads, breads and biscuits. Thyme makes a good substitute.

Mint (*Podina*)

Mint was the favourite herb of the Moghuls, who used it in their kebabs, pilafs and special lamb preparations. Spearmint is preferred to peppermint and the fresh herb to the dried. But in case of emergency, use 1 teaspoon powdered dried mint in place of 1 tablespoon finely chopped fresh mint.

Mustard Seeds (*Sarsoon*)

These tiny round seeds, brown, red and yellow in colour, look like large poppy seeds. They are added to hot oil and fried until they pop and release their fragrance into the oil. This mustard-laced oil is a prized seasoning in the cooking of the southern and eastern regions of India. There is very little difference between various types of mustard seeds, so use whichever is available.

Nutmeg (*Jaiphul*)

Moguls had a fondness for this spice and used it quite liberally in their braised lamb creations, pilafs and meat casseroles. Nutmeg is also used in puddings, chutneys and sweetmeats. Buy whole nutmegs and grate as needed.

Paprika (*Deghi Mirch*)

Paprika, powdered dried sweet red pepper, is widely used in curry making to give the sauce a wonderful deep garnet colour without making the food hot. Since its use is purely aesthetic you may omit it if it is unavailable.

(Black) Pepper (*Kali Mirch*)

India, the home of black pepper, has been using this spice since ancient times. Black pepper is used extensively in all regions of India, in all kinds of dishes, including desserts, puddings, drinks and tea infusions. It is best to buy peppercorns and grind as needed.

Saffron (*Kesar*)

Saffron, with its hypnotic fragrance and brilliant orange colour, is the most expensive spice in the world. The Moghuls of course loved it and used it in their innumerable pilafs and meat casseroles. Saffron is also a choice flavouring in desserts, puddings, sweets, chutneys and drinks. Buy only saffron threads, as only in this form is the spice in its purest form.

Tamarind (*Imli*)

Tamarind pulp, brownish-black in colour, with a distinctive sour taste (somewhat like sour prunes),

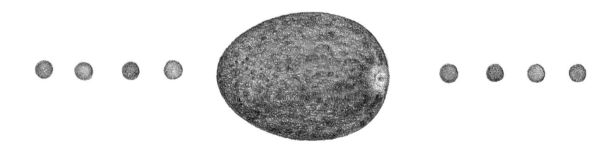

is used as a flavouring in various stews, soups, sauces and relishes. Tamarind chutney and tea infusions are very popular Indian preparations. Tamarind is sold compressed into blocks of 1 lb/ 500 g or as tamarind paste. Pitted prunes may be used as a substitute for tamarind.

Turmeric (*Haldi*)

This is the spice that colours every dish yellow. It is one of the main ingredients of curry powder. Used in moderation, turmeric provides a lovely woody scent and gives a light lemon colour to vegetables, lentils and pilafs.

SPECIAL INGREDIENTS

Flower Essences (*Ruh*)

In Indian cooking, essences of flowers, such as rose and screwpine (*kewra*), are used to provide fragrance as one uses vanilla or almond essence. These essences are not essential hence may be omitted from the recipe.

Silver Leaf (*Vark*)

This is edible paper-thin tissue of pure silver used as an adornment on foods for special occasions. It is tasteless, odourless and perfectly safe (in fact healthy) to consume. Silver leaf is available in Indian grocery stores at a very moderate cost. If unavailable just omit it from the recipe.

Usli Ghee

Many people have the incorrect notion that Indians cook all their food in *usli ghee*, Indian clarified butter. Granted that *usli ghee* has a wonderful nutty aroma, in fact it is usually reserved for flavouring lentils, rice pilafs, puddings, soups and some sweets. Most cooking is, and has for centuries been, principally done in various oils such as sesame, peanut, mustard and coconut. Concentrated or clarified butter makes a good substitute for *usli ghee*.

Usli Ghee: to make *usli ghee*, melt and simmer butter in a pan over low heat until it stops crackling and the residue at the bottom begins to turn golden brown. When cool strain the clear liquid into a jar and refrigerate or freeze. 1 lb/ 500 g butter will make 12 oz/375 g *usli ghee*.

Yogurt (*Dahi*)

Indians use yogurt in much the same way as Westerners use double cream. It is used to make sauces velvety, to mellow curries and is consumed as a drink. To prevent the yogurt from separating when added to a cooking sauce, stir a little oil (1 tablespoon for 8 oz/250 g natural yogurt) into the yogurt before cooking; it will stabilize it.

THE INDIAN MEAL

The traditional Indian style of eating is somewhat different from what is customary in the West. The Indian way of serving food is called *thali* style. Various dishes of all the courses are spooned into small individual bowls which are then neatly arranged on a large (15 in/40 cm diameter) rimmed plate or tray. Rice, bread, pickles and relishes are placed on the plate and this fully arranged *thali* is served to each person. The advantage of this style of serving is that once everyone sits down to eat the meal proceeds without interruption as all the courses have been served together.

In order to enjoy an Indian meal, of course, it is not necessary to conform to the *thali* style of eating. The Western style of serving separate courses is in fact very suitable and I find it avoids the wastage often associated with individual servings where it is hard to judge everyone's preferences and capacity.

To compose a simple meal, serve a main dish consisting of meat, poultry, fish or vegetables, and accompany it with a staple bread or rice. For a more elaborate meal, include a selection of side dishes, such as vegetables, lentils and salads. Relishes and chutneys are not essential but they certainly add texture, herbal scent and bite to the meal.

Finally, there is no reason why these dishes could not be combined with your everyday Western meal. For example serve the Chicken Curry (p. 59) simply with a nice loaf of bread and a green salad, or serve Cauliflower with Ginger (p. 70) with a fried fish. To get you started and make menu planning easier, I have given serving suggestions with each recipe.

What to drink with Indian food?

Beer and ale are the most popular alcoholic drinks served with Indian food and deservedly so, as their malty effervesence complements the fragrant aromas and complex flavours of the food beautifully. Wine lovers need not despair, however, as wine goes very well with Indian food. Any decent dry red, white or rosé will serve admirably as long as it is reasonably robust. However, your best wines should be reserved for another occasion, as their subtleties will be overpowered and lost when served with Indian food. You may of course serve non-alcoholic drinks (see pp. 89-91) as most Indians do.

Incidentally, if when eating a highly spiced dish you feel a need to extinguish the fire, reach first for some rice, bread or other starch. One or two swallows followed by a sip of iced water is much more efficient than a quaff of beer or wine!

EQUIPMENT

One wonderful aspect of Indian cooking is that there are no unfamiliar techniques that first need to be mastered nor fancy complicated gadgets to be purchased and operated. The tools and equipment found in the average English kitchen are more than adequate to perform most of the tasks required in Indian cooking.

I personally find pans with non-stick surfaces and well seasoned heavy pans particularly suitable for all-purpose cooking. Frying pans are good for vegetables, dry cooking and griddle-baked breads. A *kadhai* or a Chinese wok can prove very useful as it takes far less oil for deep frying than a deep-fryer or saucepan.

An electric spice mill or coffee mill is very handy for grinding whole spices. Finally, to make Indian cooking – or for that matter almost any cooking – child's play, invest in a food processor if you do not already own one. It can chop, shred, mince and grind, and prepare batches of perfect dough for Indian breads in a matter of seconds (see Chapter 3).

2
APPETIZERS, SAVOURIES AND SOUPS

PAPAYA SALAD

PAPEETA CHAT

A New Delhi speciality, papaya *chat* is amongst my favourite appetizers. For best results the *chat* should be assembled just before serving.

SERVES 6

1 ripe papaya	4 tablespoons finely chopped mint leaves
1 lb/500 g potatoes, boiled, peeled and cut into 1 in/2.5 cm cubes	4 tablespoons finely chopped coriander leaves
2 tablespoons lemon juice	4 green chillies, chopped
1½ teaspoons ground roasted cumin seeds	salt, to taste
	6 lettuce leaves

Cut the papaya in half, scoop out the seeds and peel carefully. Cut each half into 1 in/2.5 cm wedges and put into a bowl. Add all the other ingredients, except the lettuce leaves. Toss well. Arrange the salad on the lettuce leaves on individual plates and serve.

VARIATIONS

Use any other fruit in season in place of the papaya. Good choices would be peaches, apricots, apples, bananas, kiwifruit and slightly unripe mangoes. It is also acceptable to use them in combination.

Papaya and Pepper Salad

Substitute 1 medium green pepper and 1 medium red pepper, seeded and cut into 1 in/2.5 cm squares, for the potatoes; omit the green chillies.

FRAGRANT ONION AND COURGETTE FRITTERS

PIAZ BHOJIA

These cumin- and coriander-scented fritters, a popular North Indian snack, are excellent served with cocktails or afternoon tea. Their versatile

20

flavour allows the flexibility of serving them before any main dish.

SERVES 8 (about 32 fritters)

4 medium onions (1 lb/500 g), peeled and sliced	4 oz/125 g chick-pea flour or plain white flour
1 small courgette (4 oz/125 g), grated	2 teaspoons ground cumin
1 oz/25 g coriander leaves, chopped coarsely	1 teaspoon baking powder
2 oz/50 g natural yogurt	1 teaspoon salt
	groundnut or corn oil, for deep-frying

Put the onions, courgette, coriander, yogurt, flour, cumin, baking powder and salt in a bowl and mix, kneading the mixture until thoroughly blended.

Pour the oil into a *kadhai* or a frying pan to a depth of 2 in/5 cm. Heat to a moderate level of 375°F/190°C. Gently drop the batter mixture, in 2 tablespoonful amounts, into the oil. Make only a few fritters at a time so that there is ample room for them to float easily in the oil. Fry the fritters, turning them until they are golden brown all over (8-10 minutes). Remove the fritters with a slotted spoon and drain on kitchen paper.

VARIATIONS
Substitute 4 oz/125 g spinach, trimmed, washed and shredded, for the courgette. For hot-tasting fritters, add 2-4 chopped green chillies to the batter. *Note:* these fritters and the Broccoli and Peanut Fritters may be made ahead and kept refrigerated for up to a day. Reheat by frying in the hot oil for 30 seconds before serving.

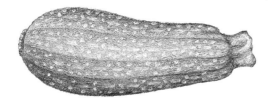

BROCCOLI AND PEANUT FRITTERS

GOBHI PAKODA

Deliciously crunchy and studded with peanuts these broccoli fritters are very popular with youngsters. Follow these spicy fritters with a subtle dish such as Tandoori Chicken (p. 44).

SERVES 8

For the batter	8 fl oz/250 ml water
6 oz/175 g chick-pea flour	½ teaspoon black pepper
2 tablespoons vegetable oil	4 oz/125 g chopped salted roasted peanuts
1½ teaspoons ground cumin	
½ teaspoon turmeric	1 medium onion, peeled and chopped
1 teaspoon mustard powder	4 tablespoons finely chopped coriander leaves
½ teaspoon baking powder	
½ teaspoon chilli powder	2 lb/1 kg broccoli, cut into florets
½ teaspoon salt	groundnut or corn oil, for deep-frying

Combine all the ingredients for the batter in a large bowl, and mix thoroughly to make a smooth batter. Add the broccoli florets and mix to coat. Pour the oil into a *kadhai* or a deep-fryer to a depth of 2½ in/6 cm. When the oil is hot (375°F/190°C) add the broccoli, a few pieces at a time, to the hot oil – do not overcrowd the pan. Fry until the coating is golden brown, turning frequently (about 5 minutes). Transfer to kitchen paper using a slotted spoon. Serve immediately.

VARIATION
Substitute a 2 lb/1 kg cauliflower for the broccoli.

BENGAL SPRING ONION-LACED FISH ROLLS

MACCHI KOFTA

A speciality of Bangladesh, these rolls can be served as a light meal accompanied by a salad. Cooked minced prawns or chicken may be used instead of the fish.

SERVES 6-8

12 oz/375 g skinless, boneless sole fillets (or use plaice or haddock), poached and flaked	*2 teaspoons lemon juice*
	2 teaspoons ground cumin
1 lb/500 g potatoes, boiled, peeled and mashed coarsely	*2 teaspoons mustard powder*
2 oz/50 g plain white flour	*½ teaspoon black pepper*
2 oz/50 g spring onions, chopped, both green and white parts	*½ teaspoon chilli powder (optional)*
	1 teaspoon salt
1 tablespoon crushed fresh ginger	*groundnut or corn oil, for deep-frying*

Combine all the ingredients except the oil in a bowl, and mix well. Pick up the mixture in 1 tablespoonful amounts and roll into neat balls. You should have about 36 1 in/2.5 cm round rolls.

Pour the oil into a *kadhai* or a deep-fryer to a depth of 2 in/5 cm. When the oil is hot (375°F/190°C) slip in a few rolls at a time, making sure not to overcrowd the pan. Fry the rolls, turning, until golden brown and crisp all around (about 3-4 minutes). Take them out with a slotted spoon and drain on kitchen paper. Serve immediately.

Fish rolls may be made ahead and refrigerated for up to 4 hours. Drop them in hot oil for 45 seconds to reheat and serve. They may also be reheated in a gas 3/325°F/160°C oven for 7 minutes.

PEPPERY ALMONDS

BHONE BADAAM

Beware of these very addictive nibbles – they go very fast and, if eaten to excess, can easily ruin the appetite. Serve before Bengal Fish in Fragrant Herb Sauce (p. 62).

SERVES 8

1 lb/500 g almonds in their skins	*½ teaspoon chilli powder*
2 teaspoons ground cumin	*½ teaspoon black pepper*
1 teaspoon salt	*groundnut or corn oil, for deep-frying*

Rinse the almonds under cold water and pat dry with kitchen paper. Mix the cumin, salt, chilli powder and black pepper in a small bowl.

Pour the oil into a *kadhai* or a deep pan to a depth of 1 in/2.5 cm. When the oil is hot (325°F/160°C) add the almonds. Stir-fry until the almonds turn several shades darker (about 5 minutes).

Transfer the almonds to a shallow dish using a slotted spoon. Immediately toss with the spices. Cool completely. The almonds will keep well for up to 2 weeks if stored in an airtight container in a cool dry place.

VARIATION

Use 1 lb/500 g cashew nuts in place of the almonds.

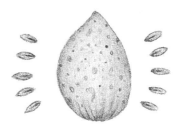

MOGHUL SAVOURY PASTRIES WITH MEAT FILLING

KEEMA SAMOSA

Samosas are delicious snacks. They also make a fine light meal served with a salad such as Carrot and Yogurt Salad with Raisins and Walnuts (p. 76).

SERVES 8-16 (makes 32 samosas)

For the dough

6 oz/175 g plain white flour, plus additional flour for dusting

1 teaspoon salt

2 oz/50 g solid vegetable fat

3½ fl oz/100 ml cold water

For the meat filling

3 tablespoons vegetable oil

1 medium onion, peeled and chopped finely

1 tablespoon finely chopped fresh ginger

1 tablespoon finely chopped garlic

1 lb/500 g lean minced beef (or lamb or a combination of the two)

1 small tomato, chopped finely

1 teaspoon salt

2 teaspoons ground cumin

½ teaspoon black pepper

2 teaspoons lemon juice

3 tablespoons finely chopped mint leaves

1 egg, beaten

groundnut or corn oil, for deep-frying

Put the flour in a large bowl. Add the salt and fat and rub into the flour. Add the water, little by little, and mix to a dough. Knead until it becomes pliable. To make the dough using a food processor, put the flour, salt and shortening into the container and run the machine until thoroughly blended. With the machine running add the water through the feed tube until a ball of dough forms on the blade. Take out the dough and gather into a ball. Cover the dough with a moist towel or clingfilm and let it rest for 30 minutes.

Make the filling. Heat a large frying pan over moderately high heat. Add the oil, ginger and garlic; then the onion and cook, stirring until the onion turns light brown (8 minutes). Add the meat, and continue cooking until the meat loses its pink colour and begins to brown. Add the tomato, salt, cumin, black pepper, lemon juice and 2 fl oz/50 ml water. Stir and bring to the boil. Lower the heat, cover and simmer for 20 minutes or until the meat is cooked and the moisture absorbed. Uncover and continue cooking until all the moisture has evaporated. Leave to cool completely and then stir in the mint and egg. The filling may be made ahead and refrigerated for up to 2 days or frozen. Defrost thoroughly before using.

Divide the dough into 2 equal portions. Roll each portion into a rope about 8 in/20 cm long and cut into 8 equal portions. Keep the dough pieces covered with a moist towel. Divide the filling into 32 equal portions.

Working with one at a time, roll each piece of dough into a thin 5 in/12 cm circle, dusting it with flour. Cut the circle in half and moisten the straight edge of each semi-circle. Make a cone of each by overlapping the straight sides together and pressing them to securely seal the joint. Place one portion of the filling in the cone, moisten the open end of the cone and quickly pinch it shut in a straight line. Make all the samosas this way. They may be refrigerated, covered, for up to a day.

When ready to cook, heat the oil in a *kadhai* or a deep-fryer to a depth of 3 in/7 cm. When the oil is hot (350°F/180°C) slip in the samosas, a few at a time, and fry until they are golden and crisp (15 minutes). Drain on kitchen paper and serve.

Note: samosas may be made ahead and kept in the refrigerator for up to 2 days. To reheat, drop them in hot oil and fry for 1½ minutes or lay them in a single layer on a baking sheet and place in a preheated gas 4/350°F/180°C oven for 10 minutes.

MULLIGATAWNY

MOLAHATANNI

Mulligatawny, basically a curried meat and vegetable soup, originated in the British Raj. There are as many interpretations of this soup as there are cooks. Here is one from Bangalore, in southern India.

SERVES 8

3 oz/75 g yellow split peas	8 medium mushrooms, chopped
4 fl oz/125 ml vegetable oil	2 oz/50 g coriander leaves, trimmed and chopped finely
3 tablespoons curry powder	1¾ pt/1 litre rich chicken, beef or lamb stock
3 medium onions, peeled and minced	
1 tablespoon crushed fresh ginger	4 fl oz/125 ml double cream
4 cloves garlic, peeled and chopped	salt and black pepper
	For the garnish
1 medium carrot, peeled and chopped finely	4 oz/125 g cooked meat (lamb, chicken or beef) (optional)
1-2 stalks celery, chopped finely	coriander sprigs

Pick clean the split peas, rinse in water and drain. Put the oil in a deep heavy pan and place it over moderate heat. Add the split peas and sauté for a few minutes. Add the curry powder, let it sizzle for a few seconds then add the onions, ginger and garlic. Sauté for 5 minutes or until the onions look soft and begin to colour.

Add the carrot, celery, mushrooms, coriander and stock. Bring to the boil. Lower the heat and simmer, covered, for 1 hour or until the peas are tender and the vegetables thoroughly cooked.

When cool, blend the soup in batches to make a smooth purée. Return the soup to the pan and gently heat through. Stir in the cream and season with salt and pepper.

When piping hot, serve in individual soup plates garnished with chopped cooked meat, if you wish, and coriander sprigs.

CHILLED MINTED YOGURT SOUP

DAHI SHORVA

An uncommonly refreshing soup that is simple and quick to make on humid summer days to beat the heat.

SERVES 4

15 oz/450 g natural yogurt

5 fl oz/142 ml soured cream

4 fl oz/125 ml cold water

2 teaspoons sugar

½ teaspoon salt

1 teaspoon ground roasted cumin seeds

2 tablespoons chopped mint leaves

1 lb/500 g small tender cucumbers

2 spring onions, trimmed and sliced finely

1 oz/25 g chopped roasted cashew nuts, pine nuts or walnuts

8 oz/250 g cooked, drained chick-peas (home-made or canned) (optional)

For the garnish

4 mint sprigs

Put the yogurt, soured cream, water, sugar, salt, cumin and mint in a large bowl and mix thoroughly.

Peel the cucumbers and cut them in half. If the seeds look hard and mature, scrape them out with a spoon, and discard. Cut the cucumbers into ¼ in/5 mm dice and add them to the yogurt.

Mix in the spring onions, nuts and chick-peas. Serve the soup in individual bowls garnished with a sprig of mint.

Roasted nuts

Put nuts in a small dry frying pan over medium heat and shake frequently (8-10 minutes). Cool completely before using.

EAST BENGAL CHICKEN SOUP

MURGH SHORBA

A real treat from the Moslems of Bengal, I find this chicken soup soothing on cold winter days.

SERVES 8

4 tablespoons vegetable oil

2 medium onions, peeled and sliced thinly

2 cloves garlic, peeled and sliced thinly

2 teaspoons ground cumin

1 teaspoon turmeric

one 3 lb/1.5 kg chicken, cut into 16 pieces

2 tablespoons shredded fresh ginger

4 green chillies, sliced

1 large tomato, sliced

2 slices lemon

2 bay leaves

2 medium peppers, cored and sliced thinly

½ teaspoon black pepper

salt, to taste

4 tablespoons finely chopped coriander leaves

Heat the oil in a deep heavy pan over high heat. Add the onions and garlic and cook, stirring, until lightly coloured (10 minutes). Sprinkle with the cumin and turmeric, mix well, then add the chicken, ginger and chillies. Sauté until the chicken is lightly seared (8 minutes).

Add the tomato, lemon, bay leaves and enough water (about 3½ pt/2 litres) to cover the chicken by at least 2 in/5 cm. Bring the contents to the boil, lower the heat and simmer, uncovered, for 2-3 hours. (The longer the soup simmers the richer the flavour will be.) Add more water as necessary during cooking.

When ready to serve, add the peppers, season with the black pepper and salt, bring the soup to the boil again, and serve in soup bowls, sprinkled with the coriander.

NEW DELHI VEGETABLE SOUP

SABZI SHORVA

Here is a lovely soup bursting with the flavour of fresh garden vegetables. It makes a delightful light meal accompanied by a piece of bread and a salad.

SERVES 8

1 small head cauliflower, stalk cut off

2 medium potatoes, peeled

4 oz/125 g fresh green beans, trimmed

4 oz/125 g carrots, peeled

4 oz/125 g shelled green peas, fresh or frozen

2 tablespoons vegetable oil

2 teaspoons cumin seeds

1 teaspoon ground cumin

1 teaspoon turmeric

½ teaspoon chilli powder

2 large tomatoes (12 oz/375 g), or 3-4 canned tomatoes, puréed

salt, to taste

For the garnish

4 tablespoons finely chopped coriander leaves

Dice the cauliflower, potatoes, beans and carrots and put in a bowl. Add the peas if fresh (do not add frozen peas now) and set aside.

Heat the oil in a deep heavy pan over moderate heat. When it is hot add the cumin seeds. When the cumin turns several shades darker (about 20 seconds) add the prepared vegetables and mix thoroughly. Add the ground cumin, turmeric and chilli powder. Stir for a minute then add the tomatoes, salt and 1¾ pt/1 litre water.

Bring to the boil. Lower the heat and simmer the soup, covered, for 30 minutes or until the vegetables are very tender. Add the frozen peas if using, and cook for 15 minutes more. Serve the soup in individual bowls sprinkled with the chopped coriander.

3
BREADS

GRIDDLE BREAD

ROTI

Roti, a wholesome and earthy-tasting wholewheat bread, is the staple of North India. *Roti* goes well with all dishes, particularly when you want a light meal.

SERVES 8

4 oz/125 g strong white flour, plus additional flour for dusting	½ teaspoon salt
	1 tablespoon vegetable oil
4 oz/125 g wholemeal flour	7 fl oz/200 ml milk or water, more as needed

Combine the flours and salt in a medium bowl. Add the oil and rub into the flour. Mix in the milk or water. Knead the dough on a lightly floured surface for 2 minutes. Cover the dough and let rest for 30 minutes. To make the dough in a food processor, blend the flours, salt and oil in the container. With the machine running, add the milk or water through the feed tube and mix until dough forms on the blade. Process for 50 seconds to knead. (The dough may be prepared ahead and set aside at room temperature for up to 8 hours or refrigerated for 5 days. Bring the dough to room temperature before using.)

Divide the dough in half. Shape each half into a rope and cut into 8 equal portions. Cover with a moist towel and set aside. Shape each portion of dough into a smooth ball and roll into a 4 in/10 cm circle, dusting often with flour to prevent sticking. Cover the rounds with a moist towel as you complete rolling them. Do not stack them.

Heat a dry frying pan or a griddle over high heat until hot. After being baked in the frying pan these breads are toasted over a gas flame or directly over an electric burner. If you use an electric burner, place a cake rack flat on the burner and set the temperature at the highest level.

Bake the breads, one or more at a time without overcrowding, for about 1½ minutes or until brown spots appear on the bottom. With tongs, turn the bread over and bake the other side for about 1 minute. Remove the bread with the tongs and place it in the flame of a gas burner or place it on the rack on a preheated electric grill. Cook for 3-6 seconds or until puffed. Turn the bread and

cook the other side for about 3 seconds. Repeat for the remaining breads.

Serve immediately, if desired, brushed with butter.

INDIAN BALLOON BREAD

POORI

One of the most beautiful breads from India, *poori*, looks like a balloon. These light airy puffs of dough go well with just about every dish, particularly those with a rich, spicy gravy.

SERVES 4

2 oz/50 g wholemeal flour, plus additional flour for dusting

2 oz/50 g self-raising flour

3 fl oz/75 ml buttermilk

groundnut or corn oil, for deep-frying

Combine the flours in a medium bowl. Mix in the buttermilk. Knead the dough on a lightly floured surface for 2 minutes. Cover and let rest for 15 minutes. To make the dough in a food processor, put both flours in the container and run the machine until the flours are blended. Add the buttermilk through the feed tube, while the machine is running, until a ball of dough forms on the blade. Process the dough for 50 seconds, turning the machine on and off every 10 seconds. Remove the dough to the work surface and keep covered with a moist towel.

Divide the dough into 8 pieces. Take 1 piece and roll into a smooth ball. Dust generously with flour and roll into a 5 in/12 cm diameter circle, dusting with flour to prevent sticking. Cover and repeat with the remaining pieces of dough. Do not stack the *poori*.

Pour the oil into a *kadhai* or deep pan to a depth of 2 in/5 cm. Heat the oil to a moderate level of 375°F/190°C. Add 1 *poori* to the oil – it will sink to the bottom. When it starts to rise, gently press it in the centre with the back of a slotted spoon until the bread puffs. Turn and cook until lightly browned (20 seconds). Transfer to kitchen paper using a slotted spoon. The bread will be light and puffed up, just like a balloon. Keep warm while cooking the remaining breads. Place on a platter and serve immediately.

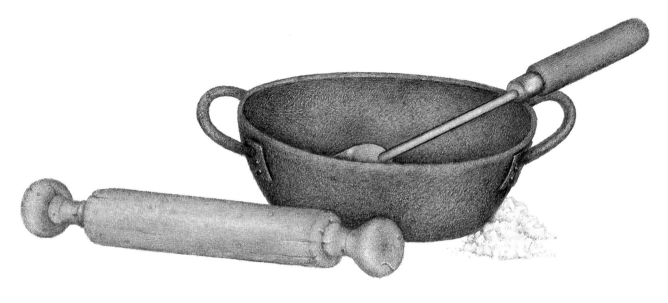

FLAKY LAYERED BREAD

PARATHA

Paratha is the Indian version of a simple puff pastry. The rich flaky layers give this bread a delicious crispness. *Paratha* is great served with vegetables and yogurt salads. For a complete meal serve it with Chicken in Butter Sauce (p. 60).

SERVES 8

6 oz/175 g chapati flour or wholemeal flour plus additional flour for dusting	*4 fl oz/125 ml vegetable oil*
	4 fl oz/125 ml warm water
½ teaspoon salt	

Combine the flour and salt in a medium bowl. Add 1½ tablespoons of the oil and rub it into the flour. Mix in the water. Knead the dough on a lightly floured surface for 2 minutes, then cover and let it rest for 15 minutes. To make the dough in a food processor, put the flour, salt and 1½ tablespoons oil into the container and process until all the ingredients are blended (about 10 seconds). Add the water through the feed tube with the machine running, until a ball of dough forms on the blade. Process the dough for 50 seconds, turning the machine on and off every 10 seconds. Remove the dough to the work surface.

Divide the dough into 8 pieces and cover with a kitchen towel.

Shape a piece of dough into a smooth ball and roll it into a 5 in/12 cm round, dusting often with flour to prevent sticking. Brush the top lightly with oil to within ½ in/1 cm of the edge and fold the round in half. Brush the top of the semi-circle with oil and fold again in half to form a triangle. Press down on the bread to flatten it slightly.

Dusting often with flour and rotating the bread, gently roll the bread, stretching it into a 6 in/ 15 cm triangle. Cover with a kitchen towel and repeat with the remaining dough. Do not stack as they will stick.

Heat a frying pan or griddle over fairly high heat until hot. Add 1 rolled bread and let it cook for 2-3 minutes on each side or until flecked with brown. Pour 1½ teaspoons of oil on and around the bread. Fry, turning, until it develops patches of brown (2-3 minutes) on each side. Remove the bread and keep warm. Cook all the breads the same way.

Note: the breads may be made ahead and set aside at room temperature until needed or refrigerated for up to 4 days. To reheat, place on a hot frying pan for a few minutes (one at a time) or in a preheated moderately hot oven, gas 6/400°F/200°C, for 4 minutes.

SPINACH BREAD

SAAG PARATHA

Extremely nutritious and flavoured with spinach this bread is among my favourites. Kale or mustard greens used in combination with spinach give an interesting flavour. Cut into wedges, spinach breads make excellent appetizers with cocktails. They go well with *tandoori* meats (see Chapter 5).

SERVES 8

6 oz/175 g chapati flour or wholemeal flour, plus additional flour for dusting	1 lb/500 g fresh spinach, trimmed, blanched, squeezed of excess water and chopped finely
½ teaspoon salt	½ teaspoon black pepper
4 fl oz/125 ml vegetable oil	3 fl oz/75 ml or more water
1 teaspoon cumin seeds	

To prepare the dough and make the bread, follow all instructions given for making *Paratha* on p. 31, except add the cumin, spinach and pepper to the flour with the salt and oil before adding the water to make the dough.

Note: if you use frozen and thawed spinach, 8 oz/ 250 g will be enough.

CAULIFLOWER AND ONION BREAD WITH CORIANDER

GOBHI PARATHA

I love this cauliflower bread because one is able to taste the delicate flavour of the vegetable. Also it is simple and quick to make. Cauliflower bread is great at picnics particularly when accompanying *tandoori* meats (see Chapter 5). For a light meal serve with Beef Frazer (p. 58) or Creamed Lentils with Fragrant Spice Butter (p. 72).

SERVES 8

For the stuffing	For the dough
1 medium cauliflower, grated coarsely	8 oz/250 g chapati flour or wholemeal flour
1 medium onion, peeled and chopped finely	4 oz/125 g self-raising flour
1½ teaspoons salt	4 fl oz/125 ml vegetable oil, for cooking bread
½ teaspoon chilli powder	8 fl oz/250 ml warm water
3 tablespoons vegetable oil	
4 tablespoons finely chopped coriander leaves	

Put the cauliflower, onion, salt, chilli powder and oil in a large frying pan. Cook the mixture over moderately high heat, stirring often, until the cauliflower looks tender and most of the moisture has evaporated (10 minutes). Turn off the heat, and stir in the chopped coriander. Cool completely. The stuffing may be made ahead and kept in the refrigerator for up to a day. Use straight from the refrigerator when ready to make bread.

To prepare the dough and bread follow all the instructions given for making Moghul Bread with Fragrant Meat Stuffing, opposite.

Moghul Bread with Fragrant Meat Stuffing

SHAHI PARATHA

Rich and filling, this royal bread with meat filling needs only a salad to complete the meal. A good choice is Mixed Vegetable Salad in Yogurt Dressing (p. 76).

SERVES 8

8 oz/250 g chapati flour or wholemeal flour, plus additional flour for dusting	8 fl oz/250 ml warm water
4 oz/125 g self-raising flour	1 recipe Meat Stuffing p. 24 (see Note below)
4 fl oz/125 ml vegetable oil	2 hard-boiled eggs, shelled and chopped finely

Put the flours in a large shallow bowl, add 1½ tablespoons oil and rub it in. Mix in the water, pouring in a stream. Gather the dough together and knead it until smooth, dusting with flour if it is very sticky (5 minutes).

To make the dough in a food processor, blend both the flours and 1½ tablespoons oil. With the machine running, add the water through the feed tube and mix until a dough ball forms, then process for 50 seconds to knead.

Whichever method you use, cover the dough and let rest for 30 minutes. The dough may be prepared and kept refrigerated for up to 5 days. Bring to room temperature before using.

Combine the meat stuffing and eggs in a small dish. Divide into 8 equal portions.

Divide the dough into 8 equal portions. Roll 1 piece between the hands into a smooth ball. Keep the remainder covered. Roll the dough ball out on a lightly floured surface to a 10 in/25 cm circle, dusting often with flour.

Place one portion of filling in the centre and spread to a 5 in/12 cm circle. Brush the dough border with water. Fold the edges into the centre forming a 5 in/12 cm circle, pleating and pressing them lightly, to seal. Cover the bread with a moist towel. Repeat with the remaining dough and filling. Do not stack them as they will stick.

Heat a frying pan or griddle over moderately high heat. When it is hot, place 1 bread in the frying pan and cook until the underside is spotted with brown (about 2 minutes). Turn and cook the other side the same way. Add 2 teaspoons of the oil on and around the bread and fry, turning a few times until thoroughly cooked and fried. Remove and keep warm. Cook the other breads in the same way.

Note: you may use any leftover meat or chicken in this recipe. If you are using minced meat from a roast chicken, beef or lamb, add 1 teaspoon ground cumin, 1 tablespoon lemon juice, 1 tablespoon chopped coriander leaves, and if desired, ½ teaspoon chilli powder or black pepper, to give the stuffing an Indian flavour.

These breads may be made ahead and set aside at room temperature for up to 6 hours or refrigerated for 2 days. Reheat in a warm frying pan for a couple of minutes, turning them, or in a preheated gas 6/400°F/200°C oven for 4 minutes.

TANDOORI BAKED BREAD

NAN

Nan is the popular bread generally seen on Indian restaurant menus. *Nan* is the obvious choice to accompany *tandoori* meats (see Chapter 5) because it is baked in the *tandoor* after the meats.

SERVES 8

12 oz/375 g strong white flour	*¾ teaspoon salt*
2 teaspoons baking powder	*7 fl oz/200 ml milk*
1½ teaspoons sugar	*6 oz/175 g unsalted butter*
	1 egg
	vegetable oil, as needed

Combine the flour, baking powder, sugar and salt in a bowl. Heat the milk with 2 oz/50 g of the butter until the milk is warm and the butter melted. Beat the egg in a large bowl. Slowly beat the milk mixture and then the flour mixture into the egg, mixing by hand just until a dough forms (the dough will be very soft, moist and sticky). Wipe your hands clean and oil them generously. Knead the dough in the bowl until smooth and satiny, oiling your fingers and the dough as necessary to prevent sticking (5-6 minutes). Cover and let it rest for 4-5 hours in a warm place.

Divide the dough into 8 equal portions and roll them into smooth rounds between your hands, oiling your hands if necessary. Cover them with a moist towel and let rest for 30 minutes. (The dough can be prepared ahead and refrigerated for up to 4 days.)

Preheat the oven to gas 9/475°F/240°C.

Stretch and pat the pieces of dough, one at a time, into 5-7 in/12-18 cm ovals. Arrange in a single layer on baking sheets and bake in the middle level of the oven for 4½ minutes or until they begin to puff and brown. Remove and, if desired, place them under the grill for 15-30 seconds to brown nicely.

Melt the remaining butter while the bread is baking. Brush each bread with the melted butter and serve immediately.

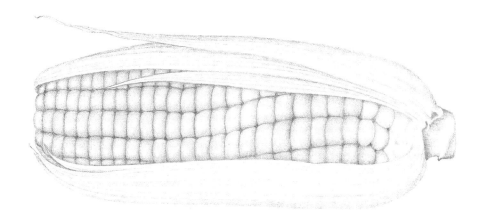

FRESH CORN BREAD

BHUTTE KI ROTI

This lovely, fragrant bread is made with puréed fresh corn and white flour. These breads go well with a cool glass of lassi (p. 89) and accompanied by a chutney or relish they make a satisfying snack.

SERVES 12

8 oz/250 g corn kernels (or use a 10 oz/300 g packet frozen corn, defrosted and squeezed of excess moisture)

⅓ teaspoon coarse salt (optional)

5 oz/150 g or more plain flour (or a combination of chapati and plain flour) plus additional flour for dusting

1 tablespoon light vegetable oil

unsalted butter (optional)

Grind the corn and salt in a food processor or blender until it is finely puréed. Transfer to a mixing bowl. Add flour a little at a time and blend until the mixture turns into a soft, sticky dough. Clean your hands thoroughly. Pour on the oil and coat the dough to prevent it from sticking.

Divide the dough into 12 equal portions. Shape each into a smooth ball and roll into a 6 in/15 cm round, dusting often with flour to prevent sticking. Cover the rounds with a tea towel as you roll them. Do not allow the rounds to touch each other.

Heat a griddle or heavy frying pan over high heat for 3 minutes. Reduce heat to medium and place one round of dough on the griddle or frying pan. Cook until the underside is spotted with brown (about 1½ minutes). Turn over; cook until the second side is spotted with brown (about 1 minute). Remove the bread and, if you wish, brush it with butter. Cover and keep warm in the oven while you cook the remaining rounds. Serve immediately.

To intensify the roasted corn flavour of the bread, after cooking it on the griddle, hold it directly over a high flame, using tongs, and toast, turning frequently, for 8-10 seconds. Do not allow it to burn. Brush with butter, if you wish, and keep warm.

4

RICE AND GRAINS

BASIC TECHNIQUES FOR COOKING PERFECT RICE

CHAWAL

Indian long grain rice called *basmati*, with its nutty fragrance, milky flavour and exquisite texture, is unmatched in the world. It is this rice that is commonly used in Indian pilafs and spice-laced casserole preparations. *Basmati* rice is widely available, so do try to get it as there is really no good substitute. In case of emergency, however, you may substitute ordinary long grain rice or Quick Cook rice (such as Uncle Ben's).

I give 3 techniques for cooking rice, each of which produces perfectly cooked rice. The first technique is similar to cooking pasta, the rice is cooked in a large quantity of boiling water until ready and then drained.

The second technique is the classic steam method. Here the rice is cooked in exactly double its amount of water, first boiled then steamed until the rice is fully cooked.

In the third technique the rice is first boiled rapidly in a large quantity of water and partially cooked, then placed in the oven and baked.

Regardless of the process chosen for cooking, *basmati* is always washed thoroughly and soaked in cold water for 30 minutes before cooking in order for the grain to expand better. *Basmati* grains are thinner than other rice grains; they have a loose inner structure and are low in starch, so soaking softens and relaxes the grains, thus reducing the amount of liquid needed and the cooking time.

BOILED RICE

SERVES 8

12 oz/375 g basmati rice or ordinary long grain rice	*2 teaspoons vegetable oil (optional)*

Wash the rice thoroughly in several changes of water and put it in a bowl. Add enough water to cover the rice by 1 in/2.5 cm. Let soak for 30 minutes. Drain.

While the rice is soaking bring a large quantity of water (3½ pt/2 litres) to the boil in a deep pan.

Add the drained rice, stir and bring to the boil again. Cook the rice for 4 minutes (10 minutes for ordinary long grain rice).

Take off the heat, and drain the rice well in a large sieve held over the sink. Transfer the rice to a heated platter and serve immediately.

Note: if you do not wish to serve the rice immediately, dribble the oil over it and gently fold to distribute it evenly. Cover and set the rice aside at room temperature for up to 8 hours or in the refrigerator for 2 days. Reheat the rice in a frying pan over moderate heat, stirring carefully, until heated through, or place in a preheated oven gas 4/350°F/180°C, wrapped in foil for 15 minutes. If the rice looks dry, sprinkle a tablespoon or two of water over it before wrapping and baking it.

BAKED RICE

SERVES 8

12 oz/375 g basmati or ordinary long grain rice	1 oz/25 g usli ghee or concentrated butter
	1/2 teaspoon salt

Preheat the oven to gas 3/325°F/160°C. Wash the rice in several changes of water. Put the rice in a bowl and add enough water to cover it by at least 1 in/2.5 cm. Soak for 30 minutes and drain.

While the rice is soaking, bring a large quantity of water to the boil. (The water should be at least 4 times the volume of the rice.) Add the rice and bring to the boil again. Stir often to ensure the rice does not settle at the bottom of the pan. Cook for 2½ minutes. Drain the rice well and put in an ovenproof casserole with a lid. Add the *ghee* or butter and salt, mix carefully, cover and bake in the middle of the oven for 25 minutes.

Remove the casserole from the oven and let it rest, covered and undisturbed, for 10 minutes. Fluff the rice with a fork, transfer it to a heated platter and serve immediately.

STEAMED RICE

SERVES 8

12 oz/375 g basmati or ordinary long grain rice	1 tablespoon vegetable oil (optional)
1/2 teaspoon salt (optional)	

Wash the rice in several changes of water. Put the rice in a bowl, add 1¾ pt/1 litre cold water and the salt. Soak for 30 minutes. Drain the rice, reserving the water.

Put the drained water and the oil in a pan and bring to the boil. Add the rice, stirring carefully with a fork to ensure that the rice does not settle at the bottom of the pan. Bring the water to the boil again. Cook the rice over medium heat, partially covered, until most of the water is absorbed and the surface of the rice is covered with several steam holes (about 10 minutes).

Cover the pan tightly and reduce the heat to the lowest point. Let the rice steam for 10 minutes. Remove from the heat and let the rice rest, covered and undisturbed, for 5 minutes before serving. Fluff the rice with a fork, transfer to a heated platter and serve.

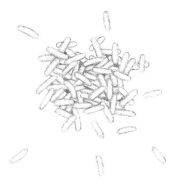

MANGO AND ALMOND PILAF

AAM PULLAO

Fruits pilafs are classic Moghul creations and the Mango Pilaf is at the top of the list. The combination of highly aromatic fruit, crunchy nuts and smooth fragrant rice provides a highly sensuous experience. Madras Fish in Fiery Tamarind Sauce (p. 63) or Malabar Prawns in Coconut Sauce (p. 65) are ideal served with it.

SERVES 6

1 large, firm, ripe mango	*¼ teaspoon ground cinnamon*
10 oz/300 g basmati rice or ordinary long grain rice	*¼ teaspoon ground cloves*
½ teaspoon screwpine essence (optional)	*¼ teaspoon grated nutmeg*
2 oz/50 g usli ghee or concentrated butter, or 4 tablespoons vegetable oil	*½ teaspoon ground ginger*
2 tablespoons sliced almonds	*4 fl oz/125 ml mango juice (fresh or canned) or other fruit juice such as peach, apricot, pear or guava*

Peel and stone the mango and cut the pulp into neat 1 in/2.5 cm cubes. Set aside.

Wash the rice thoroughly in several changes of water. Put the rice into a bowl and add enough water to cover it by at least 2 in/5 cm. Let it soak for 30 minutes.

Bring a large quantity of water (3½ pt/2 litres) to the boil in a deep pan. Add the drained rice and bring to the boil again, stirring frequently to prevent the rice from settling. Boil for 4 minutes. Drain immediately in a large sieve held over the sink. Sprinkle on the essence, if used, and set the rice aside.

Heat ½ oz/15 g of the *ghee* or butter, or 1 tablespoon oil, in a large frying pan. When it is hot add the almonds and sauté, turning and tossing, until lightly coloured (2 minutes). Remove the almonds and drain on kitchen paper. Add the remaining *ghee* to the pan along with the mango pieces. Over moderately high heat, sauté the mango, turning frequently for 3 minutes or until glazed and lightly browned. Sprinkle on the cinnamon, cloves, nutmeg and ginger, and continue frying for 30 seconds more. Remove the mixture to a plate and reserve.

To the same pan add the mango or fruit juice, bring to the boil and cook rapidly for a minute. Add the rice and mix gently but thoroughly. Lower the heat, cover and steam until the rice is fully cooked and the liquid is absorbed.

Add the sautéd mango mixture and any accumulated juices there may be. Mix carefully and cook, uncovered, until heated through. Transfer the pilaf to a heated platter and serve garnished with the sautéd almonds.

VARIATIONS

Peach and Walnut Pilaf
Substitute peaches and walnuts for the mangoes and almonds. Use peach or apricot juice as a first choice instead of mango juice.

VEGETABLE PILAF

SABZI PULLAO

An all-time favourite of the vegetarians, this is a very pretty pilaf, loaded with vegetables. For a simple meal serve it with any soup or salad.

SERVES 6

12 oz/375 g basmati rice or ordinary long grain rice	3 in/7 cm stick cinnamon
1 medium cauliflower	8 whole cardamom pods
4 oz/125 g fresh green beans	1 medium onion, peeled and chopped finely
1 medium carrot	1 tablespoon shredded fresh ginger
4 tablespoons green peas (fresh or frozen)	1 teaspoon finely chopped garlic
5 tablespoons vegetable oil	2 teaspoons salt
1 teaspoon cumin seeds	2 tablespoons chopped coriander leaves
1 teaspoon fennel seeds	2 tablespoons roasted blanched sliced almonds (optional)

Wash the rice thoroughly in several changes of water and put it in a bowl. Add 1¾ pt/1 litre water and soak for 30 minutes. Drain the rice, reserving the water.

While the rice is soaking, wash the vegetables. Break off or cut the cauliflower into 1½ in/4 cm florets. Trim the green beans and cut into 2 in/5 cm pieces. Peel the carrot and cut into ½ in/1 cm thick slices.

Heat the oil over moderately high heat in a heavy-bottomed pan. When the oil is hot add the cumin and fennel seeds. When the spices turn a little dark, add the cinnamon and cardamom. Let them sizzle for 30 seconds then add the onion, ginger and garlic. Cook, stirring often, until the onion is lightly coloured (7 minutes).

Add all the prepared vegetables and the salt, and cook, stirring, for 5 minutes. Add the rice and reserved water and bring to the boil.

Lower the heat and simmer, partially covered, until most of the water is absorbed and the surface of the rice and vegetable mixture is covered with steam holes. Cover the pan tightly, reduce the heat to the lowest level and steam for 10 minutes. Remove from the heat, and let the pilaf rest, covered and undisturbed, for 5 minutes.

To serve, transfer the pilaf to a heated serving platter, sprinkle with the chopped coriander and, if desired, the roasted almonds. Serve immediately.

Note: the pilaf may be made ahead and kept at room temperature for up to 6 hours or refrigerated for a day. Reheat the pilaf in a preheated oven gas 4/350°F/180°C in a tightly covered casserole for 30 minutes.

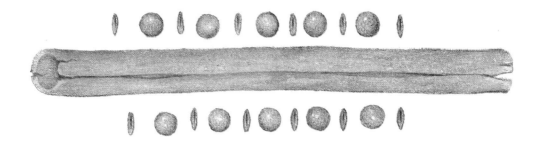

SAFFRON PILAF

ZARDA PULLAO

Delicately flavoured with saffron, raisins, sugar and cinnamon, this pilaf is a perfect accompaniment to all the royal dishes of the Moghuls.

SERVES 6

½ teaspoon saffron threads	2 oz/50 g finely chopped onion
8 fl oz/250 ml milk	1 bay leaf
12 oz/375 g basmati rice or ordinary long grain rice	¼ teaspoon ground cinnamon
1 oz/25 g usli ghee or concentrated butter, or 2 tablespoons vegetable oil	1 tablespoon sugar
	2 oz/50 g seedless raisins

Crumble the saffron threads with your finger tips and add them to the milk.

Wash the rice thoroughly in several changes of water and put it in a bowl. Add 1¼ pt/750 ml cold water and leave to soak for 30 minutes. Drain, reserving the water.

While the rice is soaking, heat the *usli ghee*, butter or oil over moderately high heat in a heavy-bottomed pan. When it is hot add the onion, bay leaf, cinnamon, sugar and raisins. Sauté until the onion looks limp and begins to colour. Add the drained rice, milk and reserved water. Stir to mix and bring to the boil. Reduce the heat and simmer, partially covered, for 10 minutes or until most of the liquid is absorbed and the surface of the rice is filled with steam holes.

Cover the pan tightly, reduce the heat to the lowest point and let the rice steam for 10 minutes. Take off the heat and let the rice rest, covered and undisturbed, for 5 minutes. Fluff the rice with a fork and serve.

SEMOLINA PILAF

OPAMA

A popular dish from South India, *opama* is made with semolina, vegetables and herbs. It is an extremely delicate pilaf with subtle flavourings, and is therefore best accompanied by spicy dishes such as Goanese Vindaloo of Duck (p. 58).

SERVES 6

5 tablespoons vegetable oil	1 medium green pepper, cored and chopped coarsely
6 tablespoons chopped cashew nuts	1½ teaspoons salt
6 oz/175 g semolina	1 pt/600 ml or more water
1½ teaspoons mustard seeds	1 medium tomato, chopped coarsely
3 oz/75 g finely chopped onion	2 teaspoons lemon juice
2 green chillies	2 tablespoons finely chopped coriander leaves
1 tablespoon finely chopped fresh ginger	6 lemon wedges

Heat 3 tablespoons of the vegetable oil in a large heavy-bottomed pan over moderately high heat. When the oil is hot, add the nuts and sauté, turning and tossing until lightly coloured (about 2 minutes). Add the semolina and fry until the grains are evenly coated with the oil and lightly fried (about 4 minutes). Transfer to a bowl and wipe the pan clean with a paper towel.

Pour the remaining 2 tablespoons of oil into the pan. When it is hot, add the mustard seeds. Keep a lid handy as the seeds may splutter and scatter. When the spluttering subsides add the onion, chillies, ginger and pepper. Fry, stirring, until the vegetables look a little limp and glazed (3 minutes). Add the semolina and nut mixture along with the salt and water.

Bring to the boil, then add the tomato. Cook the pilaf, stirring with gentle strokes (so as not to crush the tomato) until it has thickened and resembles a cream soup.

Reduce the heat, cover and let the pilaf cook for 5 minutes or until most of the moisture is absorbed and the pilaf looks like a Christmas pudding. Take off the heat and let the pilaf rest, covered, for 10 minutes to become drier and fluffier. Transfer it to a heated serving platter and sprinkle with the lemon juice and chopped coriander. Serve garnished with the lemon wedges.

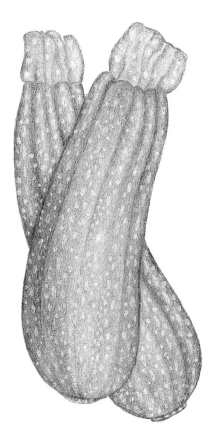

CHICKEN PILAF WITH COURGETTES

MURGH PULLAO

Here is a simple everyday rice, chicken and courgette casserole with a lovely curry flavour. All you need to complete the meal is a green salad.

SERVES 6

1 lb/500 g skinless, boneless chicken breast	8 oz/250 g natural yogurt, beaten lightly
4 fl oz/125 ml vegetable oil	2 teaspoons salt
4 oz/125 g finely chopped onion	1 recipe cooked rice (preferably basmati, day old – see pp. 36 or 37)
1 tablespoon finely chopped fresh ginger	
1 tablespoon finely chopped garlic	1-2 tablespoons milk or water (optional)
4 bay leaves	**For the garnish**
1 tablespoon curry powder	2 tablespoons roasted chopped walnuts
2 medium courgettes cut into 1 in/2.5 cm pieces	coriander sprigs (optional)

Cut the chicken into 1 in/2.5 cm wide strips. Cut each strip into ½ in/1 cm pieces. Set aside.

Heat the oil in a large heavy-bottomed pan and add the onion, ginger and garlic. Cook over moderately high heat, stirring, until the onion looks soft and begins to colour (4 minutes). Stir in the bay leaves and curry powder, mix well and add the chicken. Sauté the chicken until it loses its pink colour (4 minutes).

Add the courgettes, continue cooking and stirring, until the courgettes look slightly fried and begin to steam. Stir in the yogurt and salt. Bring to the boil. Lower the heat and cook, covered, for

42

8 minutes or until the chicken is very tender and the courgettes cooked.

Uncover and fold in the rice. Cover tightly and continue steaming until the rice is heated through and the flavours have blended (about 6 minutes). Check during cooking to ensure the pilaf is not becoming too dry and burning. If necessary sprinkle in a tablespoon or two of milk or water.

Take the pilaf from the heat and leave to rest, covered and undisturbed, for 10 minutes. Transfer to a heated platter and serve garnished with the walnuts and, if desired, the coriander sprigs.

SMOKED SALMON AND SPRING ONION KEDGEREE

KHICHDEE

A traditional Anglo-Indian brunch or luncheon dish. I think of this creamy rice as the Indian version of risotto. It can be served as a complete meal in itself accompanied by a green salad or as a side dish with *tandoori* meats (see Chapter 5).

SERVES 6

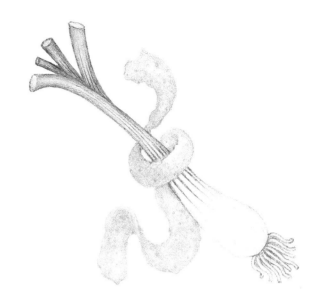

6 large eggs, size 1-2	2 oz/50 g spring onions, trimmed and chopped, both white and green parts
2½ oz/65 g unsalted butter	
1½ teaspoons salt	½ teaspoon black pepper
8 oz/250 g Quick Cook rice	4 oz/125 g smoked salmon, cut into bite-sized pieces
8 fl oz/250 ml double cream	
strip of lemon zest	**For the garnish**
pinch of grated nutmeg	coriander sprigs
1 tablespoon plain white flour	

Hard boil the eggs, peel them and put them in a bowl of cold water. Set aside until needed.

In a medium pan, combine 1 pt/600 ml water, 1 oz/25 g of the butter and 1 teaspoon of the salt. Bring to the boil and add the rice. Cover and cook, over moderately low heat, for 30 minutes or until the water is absorbed and the rice is tender. Remove the rice from the heat. Stir in 4 tablespoons of the cream and set aside, covered, for 10 minutes.

In a large pan melt the remaining butter over moderately high heat. Add the lemon zest and let it sizzle for 30 seconds. Stir in the nutmeg and flour, and cook, stirring until browned (about 1 minute). Add the remaining cream and cook until the sauce thickens. Remove and discard the lemon zest.

Stir in the remaining ½ teaspoon salt, the spring onions and pepper. Add the rice and salmon and cook, stirring until heated through.

Transfer the kedgeree to a heated serving platter or bowl. Sprinkle with the remaining black pepper, add the quartered boiled eggs, garnish with coriander sprigs and serve.

VARIATION
Prawn and Spring Onion Kedgeree
Substitute 1 lb/500 g peeled, deveined and cooked prawns for the smoked salmon.

5
TANDOORI COOKING

In India the processes of baking, roasting and grilling are done in a clay oven called a *tandoor* which is thought to have originated in Iran but today is used throughout central Asia. The Indians initially used the oven to bake bread and this is still its main use. The breads are slapped onto the sides of the *tandoor*, to which they adhere, puff up and bake. (See *Nan* p. 34) Any meat or fish that can be threaded on skewers can be cooked in *tandoor*. The skewers are lowered into the *tandoor* pit and cooked. The meat remains tender and moist because it is first marinated in spicy yogurt. I have given instructions for cooking these dishes in a conventional oven or on a grill. The unique earthy *tandoor* flavour will be lost, but the results are still very good.

TANDOORI CHICKEN

TANDOORI MURGH

Tandoori chicken is the most popular Indian restaurant dish. The meat is marinated in a spicy yogurt marinade and then cooked in the Indian clay oven called a *tandoor* where it roasts and grills simultaneously. *Tandoori* chicken is great at picnics and barbecues.

SERVES 8

two 3 lb/1.5 kg chickens, split or quartered (or use cut-up legs and breasts in any combination)

oil, for basting

For the marinade

8 oz/250 g natural yogurt

4 tablespoons vegetable oil

4 tablespoons white wine vinegar

2 teaspoons finely chopped garlic

2 teaspoons finely chopped fresh ginger

2 teaspoons black pepper

1 teaspoon chilli powder

2 teaspoons ground cardamom

1 tablespoon ground cumin

1 tablespoon red food colouring (optional)

2 tablespoons yellow food colouring (optional)

2 teaspoons salt

For the garnish

slices of onion, pepper and tomato

Pull the skin off the chicken pieces using kitchen paper to get a better grip. Prick the chicken all

over with a fork or a thin skewer. Make diagonal slashes, ½ in/1 cm deep and 1 in/2.5 cm apart, on the meat. Set aside.

Put all the ingredients for the marinade in a large bowl. Mix thoroughly using a whisk or a wooden spoon. Add the chicken and mix, turning several times to coat the pieces evenly with the marinade.

Cover and marinate at room temperature for at least 1 hour (preferably 4 hours), or in the refrigerator for at least 8 hours (maximum 2 days).

Take the chicken from the refrigerator at least 1 hour before cooking to bring to room temperature. It is now ready to be either roasted in the oven or grilled.

Preheat the oven to gas 9/475°F/240°C. Remove the chicken pieces from the marinade, shaking well to remove excess marinade clinging to them, and place them in a single layer in an extra-large shallow roasting tin preferably on a wire rack. Brush the chicken with oil and put the tin in the oven. Roast for 25 minutes or until the meat is cooked through. There is no need to baste or turn while the chicken is roasting.

To grill, place the grill pan at least 5 in/12 cm away from the heat and cook the chicken pieces, turning them often until thoroughly cooked (about 35-40 minutes).

To serve, arrange the chicken on a heated platter and surround it with slices of onion, pepper and tomato.

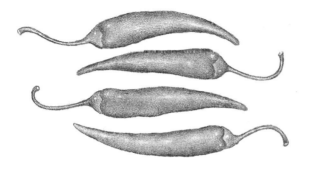

CHICKEN TIKKA GINGER KEBABS

MURGH TIKKA

Chicken kebabs are similar to *tandoori* chicken except that boneless chicken meat is used and the marinade has a pronounced ginger fragrance. Serve with Mint Chutney or North Indian Vegetable Relish (p. 80).

SERVES 8

two 3 lb/1.5 kg skinned and boned chickens, cut into 1½ in/4 cm pieces	1 teaspoon finely chopped garlic
oil, for basting	1 tablespoon ground cumin
For the marinade	1 tablespoon ground coriander
8 fl oz/250 ml soured cream	4 green chillies, chopped finely
3 tablespoons oil	1 teaspoon salt
3 tablespoons white wine vinegar	**For the garnish**
1 tablespoon crushed fresh ginger	1 medium onion, peeled and sliced
1 teaspoon ground ginger	4 oz/125 g coriander leaves, including the stalks if tender

Put the chicken pieces into a large bowl.

Blend together all the marinade ingredients in another bowl. Pour the marinade over the chicken. Stir well to coat all the chicken pieces thoroughly. Cover and marinate for 1 hour at room temperature (maximum 4 hours) or refrigerate overnight (maximum 2 days).

Take the chicken from the refrigerator. Remove the chicken from the marinade and allow it to come to room temperature before cooking. When ready to cook, preheat the oven to gas 9/475°F/240°C. Thread the chicken pieces on skewers. Brush with oil and place the skewers in a single layer in a roasting tin, preferably on a wire rack. Place the tin in the oven and roast for 10 minutes or until the kebabs are fully cooked. Do not overcook as they dry out easily.

To grill chicken, place the grill pan about 4 in/10 cm away from the heat. Brush the skewered chicken with the oil then grill, turning often, until they are fully cooked (about 6-8 minutes).

Slide the chicken kebabs off the skewers and arrange them on a heated platter. Surround them with onion slices and fresh coriander and serve.

LAMB BOTI KEBABS

BOTI KABAB

Lamb kebabs are basically cubes of lamb in a cumin- and black pepper-laced yogurt marinade, roasted or grilled to a melting tenderness. All rice pilafs (see Chapter 4) and breads (see Chapter 3) go well with these kebabs.

SERVES 6

1-1½ lb/500-750 g lean boneless lamb, cut into 1½ in/4 cm cubes

oil, for basting

For the marinade

8 oz/250 g natural yogurt

4 tablespoons vegetable oil

4 tablespoons white wine vinegar

2 tablespoons garam masala or ground cumin

2 teaspoons ground or crushed fresh ginger

1 tablespoon finely chopped garlic

2 teaspoons ground coriander

1 teaspoon chilli powder

1 teaspoon salt

For the garnish

8 oz/250 g lettuce, chopped

1 small pepper, cored and cut in matchsticks

1 medium carrot, peeled and cut in matchsticks

Place the lamb pieces, one at a time, on a work board. Using a kitchen mallet pound each one gently to break the tissues and flatten it slightly. Set aside.

Combine all the marinade ingredients in a large bowl. Add the lamb and mix, turning the meat several times to coat the pieces with the marinade. Cover and set aside for 1 hour at room temperature (maximum 4 hours) or refrigerate overnight (maximum 2 days).

When ready to cook, preheat the grill to high. Lift the meat from the marinade and thread on skewers. Brush liberally with oil and place the skewers under the grill in a single layer on an extra large baking sheet, preferably on a wire rack. Grill, turning frequently, until the lamb is cooked (about 8 minutes). It should be crusty on the outside but still pink in the middle. Baste the meat a few times during cooking.

To cook the kebabs on a charcoal grill, place the skewered oiled meat over the heat and cook, turning and basting with oil, until cooked (about 10 minutes).

To serve, slide the kebabs off the skewers on to a heated platter and garnish with the lettuce, pepper and carrot.

BEEF PASANDA KEBABS

PASANDA KABAB

These are very similar to the lamb kebabs except here the marinade is accented with cardamom and mustard. A simple green salad and plain cooked rice (pp. 36-37) will complete the meal.

SERVES 4-6

1½-2 lb/750 g-1 kg beef kebabs or top rump, cubed and trimmed of fat

oil, for basting

For the marinade

8 oz/250 g natural yogurt

4 tablespoons vegetable oil

4 tablespoons white wine vinegar

2 teaspoons finely chopped garlic

2 teaspoons ground or crushed fresh ginger

2 teaspoons ground cumin

1 teaspoon ground cardamom

2 teaspoons mustard powder

2 teaspoons black pepper

2 teaspoons salt

For the garnish

1 small lettuce, shredded

2 small tomatoes, sliced

1 small onion, peeled and sliced

Cut the steak into 3 strips, lengthways. Cut each strip into 1 in/2.5 cm pieces.

Mix all the marinade ingredients in a large bowl. Add the beef and stir to coat it with the marinade. Cover and set aside for 1 hour at room temperature (maximum 4 hours) or refrigerate overnight (maximum 2 days).

When ready to cook, preheat the oven to gas 9/475°F/240°C. Remove the beef from the marinade and thread on skewers. Brush liberally with oil and place the skewers in a single layer in an extra large roasting tin, preferably on a wire rack. Set the tin in the oven and roast for 8 minutes for medium-rare kebabs.

To cook the kebabs under a grill or over charcoal, place the grill about 4 in/10 cm away from the heat. Place the skewers on the grill and cook, turning often (about 10 minutes).

To serve, slide the kebabs off the skewers on to a heated platter and surround them with the lettuce and the tomato and onion slices.

PRAWN KEBABS

JHEENGA KABAB

These grilled prawns are a great cocktail treat. For a light meal serve a salad with them. For a more elaborate meal include a pilaf, such as Saffron Pilaf (p. 41), and Cauliflower with Ginger (p. 70).

SERVES 4-6

2 lb/1 kg large raw prawns, shelled (but leaving the tail part on) and deveined

2 medium onions, peeled and cut into 1 in/2.5 cm pieces

2 medium green peppers, cored and cut into 1 in/2.5 cm pieces

melted butter, for basting

For the marinade

1 tablespoon finely chopped garlic

1 tablespoon ground or crushed fresh ginger

3 tablespoons lemon juice

½ teaspoon chilli powder

½ teaspoon black pepper

1½ teaspoons mustard powder

1 teaspoon horseradish

1 tablespoon yellow food colouring (optional)

½ teaspoon salt

For the garnish

3 lemons, sliced

3 tomatoes, sliced

2 tablespoons finely chopped coriander leaves

To make and serve Prawn Kebabs follow all the instructions given for making Fish Kebabs (p. 49).

FISH KEBABS

MAACHI KABAB

Fish kebab is the speciality of Bengali Christians. Delicately flavoured and cooked to perfection, these kebabs are a real treat. Serve with any rice dish (see Chapter 4) and, if you wish, a vegetable such as Courgettes with Mustard Flavouring (p. 71).

SERVES 4-6

1 1/2-2 lb/750 g-1 kg skinless, boneless non-oily firm white fish such as sea bass, turbot or monkfish, cut into 1 1/2 in/4 cm cubes

2 medium onions, peeled and cut into 1 in/2.5 cm pieces

2 medium green peppers, cored and cut into 1 in/2.5 cm pieces

melted butter, for basting

For the marinade

1 tablespoon finely chopped garlic

1 tablespoon ground or crushed fresh ginger

2 tablespoons double cream

1/2 teaspoon black pepper

4 green chillies, finely chopped

1/2 teaspoon lovage seeds, crushed

1 teaspoon fresh horseradish, grated

1 tablespoon yellow food colouring (optional)

1/2 teaspoon salt

For the garnish

3 lemons, sliced

3 tomatoes, sliced

2 tablespoons finely chopped coriander leaves

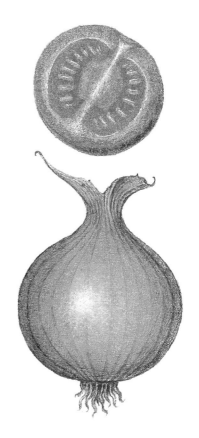

Put the fish pieces in a large ceramic bowl. Add all the marinade ingredients, and toss to coat the fish pieces evenly with the seasonings.

Cover and marinate for 30 minutes at room temperature or refrigerate overnight.

When ready to cook take the fish out of the refrigerator at least 30 minutes before cooking. Thread the fish pieces on skewers alternating with the pieces of onion and pepper.

Preheat the grill. Brush the skewered fish kebabs generously with the melted butter and place them in a single layer on a baking sheet, preferably on a wire rack. Grill, turning them once, until the fish is barely cooked (5-6 minutes).

To cook the kebabs under a grill or over charcoal, place the grill 4 in/10 cm away from the heat. Place the skewered fish, liberally buttered, on the grill and cook, turning once, basting with more butter until the fish is just cooked (8-10 minutes).

Arrange the fish still on the skewers on a heated platter. Garnish with the lemon and tomato slices, sprinkle with the chopped coriander and serve.

LAMB GRILLED WITH PAPRIKA AND MINT

BHOONA GOSHT

An Anglo-Indian speciality, this dish can also be made using goat or mutton. The leg of lamb is boned and butterflied for ease of serving. Offer Royal Peach Chutney (p. 83) or Tomato and Plum Chutney (p. 82) on the side. Any leftover meat can be sliced and served in a sandwich or combined with rice and turned into a pilaf.

SERVES 6-8

one 5-6 lb/2½-2¾ kg leg of lamb, preferably boneless

usli ghee, concentrated butter or oil, for basting

For the marinade

4 tablespoons natural yogurt

3 tablespoons finely chopped onion

4 tablespoons lemon juice

1 tablespoon finely chopped garlic

3 tablespoons shredded fresh ginger

4 tablespoons finely chopped mint leaves or 1 tablespoon dried mint

1 tablespoon ground cumin

2 tablespoons paprika

1 tablespoon black pepper

2 teaspoons salt

For the garnish

1 lb/500 g black grapes

1 bunch mint leaves

To butterfly lamb, first remove the parchment-like skin covering the leg. Remove all excess fat and place the lamb with the top side down (the side that was covered with fat) on the chopping board. If the lamb is already boned, unroll the meat, cut lengthways and open out. To bone the meat, run a sharp boning knife along the bone from the tip of the hip bone all the way down the leg, thus opening the leg and exposing the bone. Separate the bones from the meat by working around them,

scraping and pushing the meat away from the bones with the knife.

Pound the meat to an even thickness (scoring the thickest part of meat first to facilitate pounding). Prick the meat well with a fork. Transfer to a shallow roasting tin large enough for the meat to lie flat.

Mix all the marinade ingredients in a bowl. Rub the marinade on both sides of the meat. Cover and set aside for 4 hours at room temperature or refrigerate overnight (maximum 2 days). If the lamb is refrigerated, let it stand at room temperature for 2 hours before cooking.

Preheat the grill. Brush a rack set in the grill pan with melted butter or oil. Arrange the meat on the rack. Grill 2 in/5 cm away from the heat source, turning it once, until cooked to your liking, about 8 minutes on each side for medium-rare, 9 minutes for medium and 10 minutes for well done. Baste frequently with melted butter or oil. Let the lamb rest on a carving board for 5 minutes.

To roast the lamb, preheat the oven to gas 9/475°F/240°C. Arrange the lamb on a rack in a baking tin, drizzle 2-4 tablespoons of usli ghee over it and set it in the middle of the oven. Roast, without turning or basting, for 14 minutes for rare, 17 minutes for medium cooked meat. Let the lamb rest for 10 minutes, still on the rack in the pan, but out of the oven. Transfer it to a carving board.

Slice the meat across the grain into thin slices and arrange on a warm platter. Surround with small bunches of grapes and mint sprigs and serve.

INDIAN-STYLE HAMBURGERS

CHAPLI KABABS

Chapli kababs, shaped and cooked like hamburgers, are in fact a Moghul classic. They can be made with minced lamb or beef. Serve them in breads (see Chapter 3) or in hamburger rolls accompanied by a green salad.

SERVES 6

1 ½ lb/750 g extra lean minced lamb or beef

2 teaspoons garam masala

½ teaspoon black pepper

1 teaspoon salt

4 green chillies, chopped finely (optional)

4 tablespoons finely chopped mint leaves

1 teaspoon lemon juice

2 tablespoons vegetable oil

8 oz/250 g onion, chopped finely

1 tablespoon finely chopped garlic

1 tablespoon finely chopped fresh ginger

For the garnish

slices of onion, tomatoes and lettuce leaves

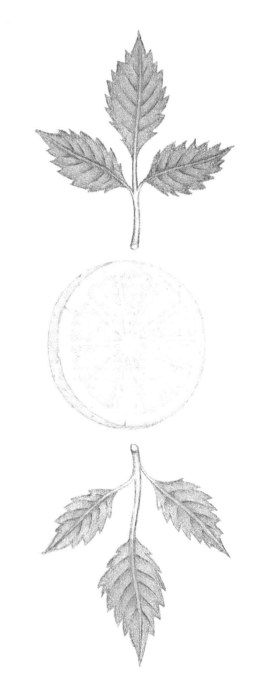

Put the meat in a bowl. Add garam masala, black pepper, salt, chillies, mint and lemon juice. Mix and set aside.

Heat the oil in a small frying pan over medium heat. When the oil is hot add the onion, garlic and ginger and cook until they begin to brown (about 15 minutes). Turn off the heat. Add the onion mixture to the meat and mix well. Divide the meat into 6 portions and form each into hamburger patties.

Preheat the grill. Brush the rack set in the grill pan with vegetable oil. Arrange the patties on the rack. Grill 2 in/5 cm away from the heat source, turning once until done – about 2½ minutes on each side for rare, 3½ minutes for medium and

4½ minutes for well done. Alternatively, the meat patties may be cooked in a frying pan for the same amount of time.

Arrange lettuce leaves on a heated platter, place the patties on them and surround with slices of onion and tomato.

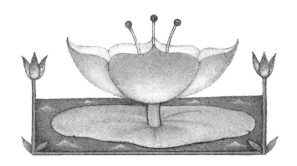

6
STEWS AND CURRIES

LAMB WITH SPINACH

SAAG GOSHT

This dish is a treat for spinach lovers – succulent pieces of lamb napped with a fragrant spinach purée. I like to serve this dish with *Paratha* (p. 31) or *Nan* (p. 34).

SERVES 6

all the ingredients for making Lamb Curry (p. 54)

1½ lb/750 g fresh spinach, cooked, or 12 oz/375 g frozen and thawed spinach

3 tablespoons vegetable oil

4 oz/125 g onion, chopped finely

2 teaspoons garam masala or ground cumin

4 green chillies, minced (optional)

Make the lamb curry following the instructions given on p. 54.

Squeeze the spinach to remove excess moisture. Coarsely chop by hand or in a food processor. Set aside.

Heat the oil in a large frying pan. When the oil is hot add the chopped onions and cook until brown (about 5 minutes). Stir in the garam masala and chillies and cook for 1 more minute. Add the chopped spinach and fry, stirring, for 3 minutes. Turn off the heat.

Add the seasoned spinach to the lamb curry, stir well to mix and serve.

VARIATIONS

Use an equal quantity of any other greens, such as mustard, kale, swiss chard or beet greens, in place of the spinach.

You may also combine several of these greens with the spinach.

Lean beef may replace the lamb.

Note: the spinach mixture and the lamb curry may be made ahead and kept refrigerated, separately, for up to 2 days. For best results, however, make the spinach the day of serving and mix with the lamb curry just before serving.

Spinach is eaten extensively in India where it is inexpensive and available all year. It can be used to flavour breads, or yogurt salads, to make dumplings or soup, or stir-fried in a fragrant oil. In this dish it is used as a sauce.

Spinach loses its flavour and its bright green colour if it is cooked with meat that contains a lot of spices, so it is cooked separately and folded into the meat at the end.

LAMB CURRY

GOSHT MASALA

The most popular of all curries, this lamb curry can be enjoyed with a bowl of rice or some bread.

SERVES 4-6

6 tablespoons vegetable oil	1 tablespoon ground coriander
1½ lb/750 g lean, boneless lamb, cut into 1½ in/4 cm pieces	½ teaspoon chilli powder
12 oz/375 g onion, chopped finely	2 teaspoons paprika
1 tablespoon ground or crushed fresh ginger	1 teaspoon turmeric
2 teaspoons finely chopped garlic	2 medium ripe tomatoes, chopped with the skins on
2 teaspoons ground cumin	1 teaspoon salt

For the garnish

4 tablespoons finely chopped coriander leaves

Heat 2 tablespoons of the oil in a large, heavy-bottomed pan over high heat until very hot. Add

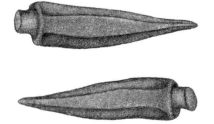

the pieces of meat and brown, turning and tossing, for 5 minutes. With a slotted spoon transfer the meat to a plate.

Add the remaining 4 tablespoons of oil and the onion to the pan and cook, stirring often, until the onion is browned (15-20 minutes). Stir in the ginger and garlic and cook 1 minute more. Stir in the cumin, ground coriander, chilli powder, paprika and turmeric until well blended. Add the tomatoes, meat, salt and 12 fl oz/350 ml water and bring to the boil.

Reduce the heat and simmer, covered, for 1½ hours or until the meat is cooked through and very tender. Turn off the heat. Serve sprinkled with the coriander.

VARIATIONS

Lamb Curry with Potatoes
Add 4-6 small, unpeeled, whole waxy potatoes (or new potatoes) during the last 30 minutes of cooking.

Lamb Curry with Courgettes
Add 8 oz/250 g courgettes sliced into 1 in/2.5 cm rounds, during the last 15 minutes of cooking.

Lamb Curry with Okra
Fry 8 oz/250 g okra, stemmed and left whole, in 3 tablespoons oil in a large frying pan until lightly browned and partially cooked (about 10 minutes). Add the fried okra to the lamb curry during the last 10 minutes of cooking.

Lamb Curry with Apricots
Sauté 1 lb/500 g ripe apricots, peeled, stoned and cut into 1 in/2.5 cm slices, in 1½ oz/40 g butter in a large frying pan until streaked with brown and glazed (about 6 minutes). Arrange the sautéd apricots on top of the lamb curry before serving.

Note: for best results let the meat rest for 30 minutes and reheat thoroughly before serving. This dish may be made ahead (in fact it tastes better the next day, like most stews) and refrigerated for up to 3 days or frozen. Defrost thoroughly and reheat slowly until piping hot.

MINCED BEEF WITH SMOKED AUBERGINE

KEEMA BAIGAN

Keema is a spicy Indian stew, similar to Mexican chilli, except that in this recipe the roasted aubergine adds a delightful and unusual fragrance. Serve a simple bread like *Roti* (p. 28) or any pilaf (pp. 39-42) with it.

SERVES 6

2 aubergines (about 1 lb/500 g each), roasted (see below)	½ teaspoon chilli powder
6 tablespoons vegetable oil	2 lb/1 kg extra lean minced beef
12 oz/375 g onion, chopped	1½ lb/750 g ripe tomatoes, cut into 1 in/2.5 cm wedges
1 tablespoon finely chopped garlic	1 teaspoon salt
3 tablespoons ground coriander	2 tablespoons lemon juice
1 tablespoon ground cumin	**For the garnish**
	2 tablespoons finely chopped mint leaves

Roast, peel and chop the aubergines (see below).

Put the oil in a large heavy-bottomed pan with the onion and garlic. Cook over moderately high heat, stirring occasionally, until the onion is browned (20 minutes).

Stir in the coriander, cumin and chilli powder. Add the beef and cook until the meat loses its pink colour (about 5 minutes). Add 8 fl oz/250 ml water and bring to the boil. Lower the heat and simmer, covered, until the meat is tender and spongy (about 30 minutes).

Fold in the roasted aubergine, tomatoes, salt and lemon juice, and continue cooking, covered, for another 5 minutes. Turn off the heat and transfer into a serving dish. Sprinkle with the mint and serve.

Roasted Aubergine

Place the aubergines, one at a time, on the burner of a gas stove, at first stem side up then laying them on their sides, turning them every minute with a pair of tongs until they are fully charred and very soft (about 15-20 minutes). When fully cooked the aubergines will be quite limp, the skin blistered, and the juices beginning to ooze out.

Let the aubergines cool briefly then carefully scrape the charred skin off. Rinse quickly under running cold water to clean the flesh of any clinging charred pieces. Pat dry on kitchen paper. Coarsely chop the pulp with a knife and put it in a bowl, cover and set aside until needed.

Note: the roasted aubergine and the beef may be made ahead and kept refrigerated separately for up to 2 days or frozen. Defrost thoroughly before combining them with the tomatoes, salt and lemon juice.

LAMB OR GOAT BRAISED IN MINT-LACED MILK SAUCE

AAB GOSHT

A truly glorious preparation, this Moghul speciality is from Pakistan. *Aab Gosht* is best enjoyed with a fragrant pilaf such as Vegetable Pilaf (p. 40) or Mango and Almond Pilaf (p. 39).

SERVES 6

8 fl oz/250 ml milk

1 medium onion, peeled and quartered

2 × 1 in/5 × 2.5 cm piece fresh ginger

3 tablespoons blanched almonds

2 teaspoons ground cardamom

1/4 teaspoon grated nutmeg

1/4 teaspoon ground cinnamon

1/4 teaspoon ground cloves

2 lb/1 kg lean, boneless lamb or goat, cut into 1 1/2 in/4 cm pieces

1 teaspoon salt

2 tablespoons finely chopped mint leaves

2 tablespoons finely chopped coriander leaves

3 tablespoons usli ghee, concentrated butter or vegetable oil

2 large cloves garlic, peeled and sliced thinly

1/2 teaspoon coarsely ground black pepper

4 fl oz/125 ml double cream, if needed

Put the milk, onion, ginger and almonds into the container of an electric blender. Run the machine until the contents are liquified. Mix in the cardamom, nutmeg, cinnamon and cloves.

Put the puréed mixture with the meat and salt into a large heavy-bottomed pan (preferably one with a non-stick surface). Place the pan over moderately high heat and bring to the boil.

Lower the heat and simmer, covered, for 1 1/2 hours or until the meat is tender. Check often and stir to ensure the meat is not sticking to the bottom of the pan and burning.

Stir in the mint, chopped coriander and a tablespoon of butter, *ghee* or oil. Set aside, covered, for 30 minutes for the flavours to blend.

Heat the remaining *ghee*, butter or oil in a small frying pan over moderate heat. Add the garlic and sauté until the slices are barely coloured (2 minutes). Stir in the black pepper and immediately pour the entire contents over the meat. Mix thoroughly. Stir in some or all of the cream if the dish looks too thick or if the sauce needs richer flavour. Heat thoroughly before serving.

LAMB CURRY WITH BRUSSELS SPROUTS

MUTTON KARIAUR GOBHI

This curry, fairly simple and quick to make, is an Anglo-Indian classic. Brussels sprouts are a pleasant addition, giving the curry a very earthy, wholesome taste. A simple green salad and some bread will complete the meal.

SERVES 6

2 lb/1 kg lean, boneless lamb, cut into 1½ in/4 cm cubes

1½ oz/40 g plain white flour

5 tablespoons vegetable oil

4 tablespoons curry powder

½ teaspoon black pepper

8 oz/250 g onion, chopped finely

1 tablespoon finely chopped garlic

1 tablespoon cider vinegar

1½ teaspoons prepared mustard

½ teaspoon salt

2 tablespoons tomato ketchup

8 fl oz/250 ml chicken stock (home-made or canned)

2 lb/1 kg Brussels sprouts, trimmed

4-5 tablespoons double cream

Pat dry the meat on kitchen paper and dust evenly with the flour.

Heat the oil in a large heavy-bottomed pan. Add the meat to the oil and sauté over high heat, turning, until browned on all sides (5 minutes). Stir in the curry powder and black pepper, and cook for 1 minute more.

Add the onion, garlic and vinegar, and cook, stirring occasionally, until softened (about 4 minutes). Now stir in the mustard, salt, ketchup and stock, and bring to the boil. Reduce the heat to moderate, cover the pan and simmer, stirring occasionally, for 45 minutes.

Add the Brussels sprouts, mix, and continue cooking, covered, for an additional 20 minutes or until the vegetables are cooked but still firm. Turn off the heat and set aside until ready to serve. Stir in the cream, simmer gently until heated through, and serve.

VARIATIONS

Lamb Curry with Carrots
Add 1½ lb/750 g carrots, peeled and cut into 1 in/2.5 cm long pieces, during the last 25 minutes of cooking. Omit the Brussels sprouts.

Lamb Curry with Pumpkin
Add 2 lb/1 kg pumpkin, seeded and cut, with the skin (if the skin is tender), into 1½ in/4 cm pieces, during the last 15 minutes of cooking. Omit the Brussels sprouts.

Note: for a milder curry reduce the curry powder to 3 tablespoons. This curry may be made ahead and refrigerated for up to 2 days or frozen. Defrost thoroughly before reheating.

BEEF FRAZER

JHAL FRAZI

Created during the British Raj and named after Colonel Frazer, Beef Frazer is a sauté of leftover roast meat with vegetables that makes a great buffet dish. It is ideal served at lunch accompanied by plain cooked rice and a vegetable such as Curried Aubergine with Chutney (p. 69).

SERVES 2

12 oz/375 g roast beef, leftover from any recipe	1 medium onion, sliced thickly
1 teaspoon ground cumin	1 large tomato, sliced
1 teaspoon curry powder	1 teaspoon prepared mustard
4 tablespoons chicken stock or water	½ teaspoon black pepper
3 oz/75 g unsalted butter	2 tablespoons finely chopped coriander leaves
	salt (optional)

Cut the beef into thick strips. Sprinkle with the cumin and curry powder and rub in. If the beef looks dry, dribble over a few tablespoons of the stock to moisten it a little and toss well.

Heat the butter in a large frying pan over moderately high heat. When the butter melts add the beef and sauté, turning for a minute. Add the onion and continue to sauté until the slices look glazed and begin to turn soft (3 minutes). Increase the heat to high and add the tomato, mustard and pepper. Sauté, tossing, until the tomato slices are barely cooked and the dish takes on a seared look (about 4 minutes).

Remove from the heat, transfer to a platter, sprinkle with chopped coriander and serve, seasoned with salt if desired.

GOANESE VINDALOO OF DUCK

VINDALOO

A speciality of Goanese Christians of Portuguese descent, *vindaloo* is a very hot and spicy curry flavoured with chilli powder, the spice the Portuguese introduced to India.

Vindaloo is best enjoyed with plain cooked rice or a loaf of bread and accompanied by a yogurt salad (see Chapter 8).

SERVES 4

one 5 lb/2.5 kg duck	2 teaspoons mustard powder
4 tablespoons mustard oil or vegetable oil	1 tablespoon chilli powder
8 oz/250 g onion, chopped finely	2 tablespoons paprika
1 tablespoon finely chopped garlic	2 tablespoons white wine vinegar
2 tablespoons ground or crushed fresh ginger	1 teaspoon tamarind paste or 3 pitted prunes, chopped finely
¾ teaspoon ground cinnamon	¾ pt/450 ml hot water
½ teaspoon ground cloves	2 teaspoons salt
1½ teaspoons turmeric	1 teaspoon jaggery or brown sugar

Split the duck in half and remove the skin and all visible fat using kitchen paper to get a better grip.

Heat 2 tablespoons of the oil in a large heavy-bottomed pan. When the oil is hot add the duck halves and cook, turning them, until they lose their pink colour (about 5-8 minutes). Take them out with a slotted spoon and transfer to a bowl.

Add the remaining oil to the same pan with the onion. Cook, stirring occasionally, until the onion turns dark brown (20 minutes). Add the garlic and ginger, and cook for another minute. Stir in the cinnamon, cloves, turmeric, mustard, chilli powder and paprika and let the spices fry for a minute.

Return the duck halves to the pan along with the vinegar, tamarind or pitted prunes, water, salt and jaggery or sugar. Bring to the boil. Lower the heat and cook, covered, for 1¼-1½ hours or until the duck is very tender. Turn off the heat, skim off excess fat and serve.

VARIATIONS

Pork Vindaloo
Use 4 pork chops (2 lb/1 kg), trimmed of excess fat, in place of the duck. Increase the cooking time to 1¾ hours.

Chicken Vindaloo
Replace the duck with 8 skinless chicken thighs (2 lb/1 kg) and reduce the cooking time to 45 minutes.

Beef or Lamb Vindaloo
Use 2 lb/1 kg lean, boneless beef or lamb, cut into 1½ in/4 cm cubes, in place of the duck. Increase the cooking time to 1¾ hours.

Fish Vindaloo
Replace the duck with 4 cod steaks, 1½ in/4 cm thick. Cook the sauce alone for 15 minutes, then sauté the fish steaks and add them during the last 6-8 minutes of cooking.

Vegetable Vindaloo
Replace the duck with 2½ lb/1.25 kg mixed vegetables (cauliflower, carrots, green beans, green peas, turnips, mange-touts, aubergine and potatoes), cut into 2 in × 1 in/5 cm × 2.5 cm pieces. Reduce the cooking time to 30 minutes.

Note: the *vindaloo* may be prepared ahead and refrigerated for up to 4 days or frozen. The flavours in fact improve with keeping. It is also easier to remove excess fat when the dish is cold. Defrost thoroughly before reheating.

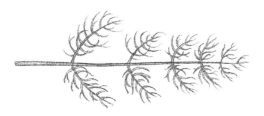

CHICKEN CURRY

MURGH MASALA

This chicken curry, fragrant with cumin and fresh coriander, is a Punjabi speciality from North India. It can also be made with partridge, duck, pheasant or pigeon.

SERVES 4-5

one 3 lb/1.5 kg chicken, cut into 8-10 pieces

6 tablespoons vegetable oil

12 oz/375 g onion, chopped finely

2 tablespoons ground or crushed fresh ginger

1 tablespoon finely chopped garlic

2 teaspoons ground cumin

1 teaspoon ground fennel

1 tablespoon paprika

1½ lb/750 g ripe tomatoes, chopped with the skins on

1½ teaspoons salt

6 fl oz/175 ml hot water

4 tablespoons single cream (optional)

For the garnish

3 tablespoons vegetable oil

4 tablespoons shredded fresh ginger

1 teaspoon (or more) black peppercorns, cracked

4 tablespoons coarsely chopped walnuts

4 tablespoons finely chopped coriander leaves

Pull the skin away from the chicken pieces, using a kitchen towel to get a better grip.

Heat 3 tablespoons of the oil in a large heavy-bottomed pan until very hot. Add the chicken pieces and sauté, turning them until they lose their pink colour (5 minutes). Remove the chicken with a slotted spoon and set aside on a plate.

Add the remaining oil to the same pan along

with the onion and cook, stirring occasionally, until the onion is lightly browned (about 20 minutes). Stir in the ginger, garlic, cumin, fennel and paprika, and cook for 1 minute more. Add the tomatoes and salt, stir well to mix, then add the chicken pieces and the hot water and bring to the boil.

Reduce the heat and simmer, covered, until the chicken is very tender (about 40 minutes). Turn off the heat, stir in the cream if using and set aside.

When ready to serve, heat the curry thoroughly and transfer to a warm serving dish. Heat a small frying pan for the garnish over high heat for 3 minutes. Add the oil and as soon as it is hot, turn off the heat. Add the ginger, black peppercorns and walnuts. Let them sizzle in the hot oil for 30 seconds. Pour the entire contents of the pan over the chicken, distributing them evenly to cover the curry with the seasonings. Sprinkle with the chopped coriander and serve.

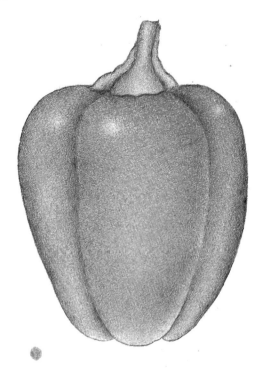

CHICKEN IN BUTTER SAUCE

MAKKHANI MURGH

Butter chicken is made by braising pieces of *tandoori* chicken in a creamy tomato sauce. Because of its mellow flavour, butter chicken is popular with all ages.

SERVES 8

all the ingredients for making Tandoori Chicken (p. 44) or 2 roast chickens (about 3 lb/1.5 kg each)	*8 fl oz/250 ml double cream*
For the sauce	*1 tablespoon ground or crushed fresh ginger*
4 oz/125 g unsalted butter	*2 teaspoons ground cumin*
1 pt/600 ml tomato purée, fresh or canned	*½ teaspoon black pepper*
	½ teaspoon salt
	7 tablespoons finely chopped coriander leaves

Make the Tandoori Chicken following the instructions. If you are using roast chickens cut them into 6-8 pieces each.

In a large shallow pan put all the ingredients for the sauce except the coriander and simmer, uncovered, for 10 minutes or until slightly thickened. Add the chicken pieces and continue cooking, uncovered, until they are heated through and have absorbed some of the sauce (about 10 minutes). Fold in the chopped coriander and serve.

Note: this dish may be made ahead and kept refrigerated for up to 2 days. Heat thoroughly and check seasonings – if necessary add more pepper and chopped coriander. For a hotter-tasting dish, fold 4 finely chopped green chillies into the sauce along with the coriander.

COUNTRY CHICKEN

Another Anglo-Indian speciality, you can also make this dish with leftover roast duck or goose.

SERVES 2

12 oz/375 g roast chicken meat (from Tandoori Chicken, p. 44, Chicken Tikka Ginger Kebabs, p. 46, Roast Chicken in Plum Sauce with Cinnamon, p. 61, or leftover roast chicken from any other recipe, skin removed)

1 teaspoon finely chopped garlic

2 medium onions, chopped finely

2 teaspoons curry powder

1/4 teaspoon ground cinnamon

2 oz/50 g unsalted butter

1 green pepper, cored and cut into 1/2 in/1 cm strips

1 red pepper, cored and cut into 1/2 in/1 cm strips

1 tablespoon tomato purée

2 tablespoons double cream

1 tablespoon lemon juice

4 tablespoons chopped coriander leaves

Cut the chicken into thick strips, put in a bowl and sprinkle with the garlic, onion, curry powder and cinnamon. Toss to mix.

Heat the butter in a large frying pan over high heat. When the butter melts add the chicken mixture and sauté, turning and tossing, until the onion begins to brown and the contents look glazed (4 minutes). Reduce the heat a little and add the pepper strips. Continue sautéing for an additional 2 minutes or until the peppers are barely cooked.

Add the tomato purée, cream, lemon juice and half the coriander. Mix thoroughly, and cook until heated through. Transfer to a serving platter and garnish with the remaining chopped coriander.

ROAST CHICKEN IN PLUM SAUCE WITH CINNAMON

MURGHI ROOSHT

Gloriously glazed to a rich red-brown, this cinnamon-scented roast chicken can form the centrepiece of the most Western of dinners. It goes very well with Mango and Almond Pilaf (p. 39) or Smoked Salmon and Spring Onion Kedgeree (p. 43).

SERVES 4

one 3-3 1/2 lb/1 1/2-1 3/4 kg roasting chicken

8 oz/250 g shallots, peeled

1 1/2 lb/750 g purple plums, stoned and cut into 1 in/2.5 cm pieces

1 in/2.5 cm cube fresh ginger

2 teaspoons paprika

1/2 teaspoon ground cinnamon, plus extra for garnish

1/4 teaspoon ground cloves

1/4 teaspoon grated nutmeg

4 tablespoons sugar

3 1/2 oz/90 g unsalted butter, melted

1 tablespoon lemon juice

salt and black pepper, to taste

Rinse the chicken inside and out, pat dry with kitchen paper and truss it.

Put 3-4 shallots, half the plums and the ginger into the container of an electric blender. Run the machine to purée the contents. Add the paprika, cinnamon, cloves, nutmeg and 3 tablespoons of the sugar and blend in.

Pour the contents into an enamelled pan and bring to the boil. Simmer the sauce, uncovered, until slightly thick and glazed like jam (15 minutes). Turn off the heat. Stir in 2 tablespoons of the melted butter, the lemon juice, salt and pepper. Set aside until needed or refrigerate (it may be refrigerated for up to 2 weeks).

Preheat the oven to gas 5/375°F/190°C.

In a large frying pan, melt the remaining butter over moderately high heat. Add the remaining whole shallots and fry, tossing frequently, until they are browned and almost tender (10 minutes). Add the remaining plums and cook, tossing, until coated with butter and heated through. Set aside to cool.

Pour a cup of water into a shallow roasting tin. Set the chicken on its side on a rack in the tin. Place in the oven and roast for 30 minutes, turning every 10 minutes; first to the other side, then breast up.

Reduce the oven temperature to gas 3/325°F/160°C. Baste the chicken with the spice and plum mixture. Continue roasting, turning occasionally and basting frequently, until the chicken is deep garnet coloured and tender (about 30 minutes longer).

To serve, place the roast chicken on a large heated serving platter. Remove the trussing string and discard. Warm the shallot and plum mixture. When hot sprinkle the remaining sugar over and fry, turning and tossing, until the sugar melts and the shallots and plums look glazed. Arrange them around the chicken and serve sprinkled with cinnamon.

For easier serving the chicken may be split in half and then arranged on the platter.

BENGAL FISH IN FRAGRANT HERB SAUCE

MAACH BHAJA

This is an everyday Bengali preparation from eastern India. It is a light dish with a great herbal fragrance. Plain cooked rice (p. 36) is the best choice to accompany this dish.

SERVES 4

4 cod, haddock or tuna steaks	12 oz/375 g onion, sliced
½ teaspoon turmeric	1 tablespoon sliced garlic
½ teaspoon chilli powder	4-8 chillies, sliced lengthways
1 teaspoon mustard powder	2 teaspoons ground cumin
3 tablespoons mustard oil or vegetable oil	1 tablespoon paprika
For the sauce	1 teaspoon salt
3 large tomatoes (about 1½ lb/750 g)	8 tablespoons finely chopped coriander leaves
6 tablespoons mustard oil or vegetable oil	juice of 1 lemon

Place the fish steaks on a plate. Mix the turmeric, chilli powder and mustard in a small dish and rub this spice mixture over the fish. Set aside.

Heat the oil in a large pan, preferably one with a non-stick surface. When the oil is hot add the fish steaks and brown, turning once (about 3-4 minutes). Return to the plate and put aside.

Purée 2 of the tomatoes using an electric blender or a food processor. Slice the third tomato. Set aside.

Add the oil for the sauce to the pan along with the onion, garlic and chillies. Cook over moderate heat, stirring occasionally, until the onion looks

MADRAS FISH IN FIERY TAMARIND SAUCE

MEEN KARI

Here is a dish for you to try if you have never cooked with tamarind before. This fish preparation from the southern shores of India gets its lovely herbal flavour and sweetish-sour taste from the tamarind. Serve plain cooked rice (p. 36) and Mango and Yogurt Salad (p. 77) on the side.

SERVES 6

6 sole fillets (about 6 oz/175 g each), skinned

1 teaspoon finely chopped garlic

2 tablespoons lemon juice

1/2 teaspoon salt

oil, for shallow-frying

plain white flour, for dusting

For the sauce

3 medium tomatoes (about 12 oz/375 g)

6 green chillies

1 1/2 in/4 cm cube fresh ginger, peeled

3 tablespoons grated fresh coconut, desiccated coconut or shavings from a block of coconut cream

2 tablespoons blanched almonds

3 1/2 fl oz/100 ml water

4 tablespoons sesame or vegetable oil

1 1/2 teaspoons mustard seeds

2 teaspoons ground coriander

1/2 teaspoon turmeric

1 teaspoon tamarind paste

3 pitted prunes, chopped finely

Place the fish fillets in a large shallow dish. Combine the garlic, lemon juice and salt and rub over the fish. Set aside to marinate for 30 minutes, or cover and refrigerate overnight (it may be left in the refrigerator for up to 2 days).

Put the tomatoes, chillies, ginger, coconut and

limp and begins to brown. Stir in the cumin, paprika and salt, let sizzle for a minute, then add the puréed tomatoes. Continue cooking, uncovered, until the sauce thickens a little (about 5 minutes).

Put in the fish and sliced tomato, and cook, turning them in the sauce, until the fish is cooked (8 minutes). Add 6 tablespoons of the chopped coriander and the lemon juice, and mix, turning the fish steaks a few times to coat them with the herb.

Remove from the heat and transfer to a warm platter. Serve sprinkled with the remaining chopped coriander.

almonds into the container of an electric blender or food processor. Run the machine until the contents reduce to a purée. Stir in the water and set aside.

Heat the oil for the sauce in a medium pan over moderately high heat. When the oil is hot add the mustard seeds. Keep a lid handy, as the seeds may splutter. When they stop spluttering add the coriander and turmeric. Let the spices sizzle for a second and immediately pour in the puréed tomato mixture. Stir in the tamarind and prunes and bring to the boil. Lower the heat and simmer the sauce, partially covered, for 20 minutes. Keep the sauce warm while you cook the fish fillets.

Heat oil to a depth of ½ in/1 cm in a large frying pan. Dust 2 or 3 fish fillets lightly with some of the flour and gently place them in the frying pan. Over moderately high heat, cook the fish, turning them once until barely done (about 1½ minutes). Remove and keep the fish warm while you repeat with the remaining fillets.

To serve place the fish fillets on individual plates. Pour 4-5 tablespoons of sauce over each and serve.

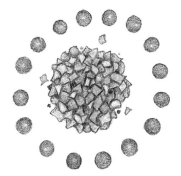

PRAWNS IN CREAM SAUCE

MALAI JHEENGA

Another Bengali preparation from eastern India, Prawns in Cream Sauce gets its lovely flavour and texture from the coconut. Saffron Pilaf (p. 41) or Spinach Bread (p. 32) are ideal served with it.

SERVES 4

1 lb/500 g medium prawns, shelled and deveined	1 teaspoon ground cumin
8 tablespoons vegetable oil	2 teaspoons ground coriander
8 oz/250 g onion, chopped finely	½ teaspoon turmeric
3 in/7.5 cm stick cinnamon	4 green chillies, minced
2 bay leaves	8 fl oz/250 ml coconut milk or single cream
1 teaspoon finely chopped garlic	1 teaspoon salt
1 teaspoon ground or crushed fresh ginger	2-3 tablespoons double cream

If you buy raw prawns, cook them until they curl loosely (about 1 minute) in a pan of boiling salted water. Drain and set aside. If the prawns are already cooked, omit this step.

Heat the oil in a medium pan and add the onion, cinnamon and bay leaves. Cook over moderately high heat, stirring occasionally, until the onion is brown (about 15 minutes). Stir in the garlic, ginger, cumin, coriander and turmeric, and cook for 2 minutes. Add the chillies and coconut milk and bring to the boil.

Reduce the heat and simmer, partially covered, for 10 minutes. Add the prawns, salt and double cream. Continue cooking until the sauce is bubbling hot, then serve at once.

MALABAR PRAWNS IN COCONUT SAUCE

MOOLEE

I simply adore this dish from Malabar in southern India. A coconut sauce with fresh ginger, green chillies and cumin is used to poach juicy prawns – the result is sublime. Serve with Semolina Pilaf (p. 41) and Madras Mushrooms with Curry (p. 71) for a complete meal.

SERVES 6

5 tablespoons sesame or vegetable oil

1 teaspoon mustard seeds

1 teaspoon finely chopped garlic

2 medium onions, chopped finely

2 tablespoons shredded fresh ginger

2 green chillies, minced

1 1/2 teaspoons ground cumin

1 pt/600 ml coconut milk

1 teaspoon salt

2 lb/1 kg medium prawns, peeled, deveined and cooked

For the garnish

2 tablespoons chopped coriander leaves

Heat the oil in a large heavy-bottomed pan over moderately high heat for 3 minutes. Add the mustard seeds. Keep a lid handy as the seeds may splutter. When the seeds stop spluttering, add the garlic and onion. Cook, stirring occasionally, until they look limp and begin to colour (about 6 minutes). Stir in the ginger, chillies and cumin, and cook for another minute.

Add the coconut milk and salt, and bring to the boil. Lower the heat and simmer, partially covered, for 8 minutes. Add the prawns and continue cooking, uncovered, stirring occasionally, until they are just heated through (about 3 minutes). Transfer to a serving dish and sprinkle with the chopped coriander.

7

VEGETABLES AND PULSES

GREEN BEANS IN GARLIC OIL

SEM BHAJI

Wonderful with *tandoori* meats, this dish is also good served cold with drinks.

SERVES 4

3 tablespoons vegetable oil	¼ teaspoon turmeric
4 large cloves garlic, peeled and sliced thinly	½ teaspoon salt
2 green chillies, sliced	4 fl oz/125 ml hot water
1 lb/500 g fresh green beans, trimmed	1¼ teaspoons prepared mustard

Heat the oil in a large heavy-bottomed pan over high heat for 3 minutes. Reduce the heat and add the garlic and chillies. When the garlic begins to turn light golden (30 seconds), add the beans, sprinkle in the turmeric and salt and mix, turning the beans to coat them evenly (5 minutes). Add the hot water, cover, and let the beans cook until tender but not mushy (10-12 minutes).

Uncover, stir in the mustard and increase the heat to evaporate excess moisture. Fry the beans, turning and tossing, until they look lightly brown and glazed. Serve hot, at room temperature or chilled.

VARIATIONS

Green Beans and Potatoes in Garlic Oil
Replace 4 oz/125 g green beans with 4 oz/125 g potatoes, cut into sticks to resemble the beans.
Green Beans and Carrots in Garlic Oil
Replace 4 oz/125 g green beans with 4 oz/125 g carrots cut into sticks to resemble the beans.
Shredded Cabbage in Mustard-Garlic Oil
Substitute 1 small cabbage about 1-1¼ lb/500-625 g for the green beans. Cut the cabbage in half and cut out the central stalk from each piece and shred the cabbage into ¼ in/5 cm shreds.

Note: for a hotter dish increase the number of chillies to 6.

CAULIFLOWER, CARROTS AND BEANS IN ALMOND SAUCE

SABZ KORMA

A speciality of the Hindu Brahmins, this vegetarian main dish casserole would please anyone, vegetarians and non-vegetarians alike. It can be served as a complete meal in itself accompanied by a green salad or a yogurt salad (see Chapter 8).

SERVES 6

1 medium cauliflower (about 1½ lb/750 g)	2 × 1 in/5 × 2.5 cm piece fresh ginger, peeled
8 oz/250 g fresh green beans	3 green chillies
12 oz/375 g baby carrots	1 tablespoon coriander seeds
12 oz/375 g shelled green peas (fresh or frozen)	7 tablespoons vegetable oil
3 oz/75 g blanched almonds, sliced or slivered	½ teaspoon turmeric
	4 fl oz/125 ml tomato purée (canned or fresh)
4 oz/125 g coriander leaves, including stalks if tender	1 tablespoon paprika
	1 teaspoon salt
	¾ pt/450 ml water

Cut off stalk and separate cauliflower into 2 in/5 cm florets. Snap off the ends of the green beans, leaving them whole. Peel the carrots. Leave them whole if they are very tiny, otherwise cut them into 1 in/2.5 cm pieces. Set aside.

Put half the almonds, half the coriander leaves, the ginger, chillies and coriander seeds into the container of an electric blender or food processor. Run the machine until the contents are finely minced. Set aside.

Heat 6 tablespoons of the oil in a large heavy-bottomed pan over moderately high heat for 2 minutes. Add the turmeric and the almond and herb mixture and fry for 3 minutes. Add the tomato purée, paprika and salt. Mix, then fold in all the vegetables. Add the water and bring to the boil. Lower the heat and simmer, covered, until the vegetables are tender but not mushy (30 minutes). Turn off the heat and let the dish rest, covered, for 15 minutes so that the flavours blend.

While the dish is resting prepare the final flavouring. Finely chop the remaining coriander leaves. Heat the remaining tablespoon of oil in a small frying pan. Add the remaining almonds and sauté, turning and tossing over moderate heat until they turn light golden (2 minutes). Add the chopped coriander and shake the pan to fry the herb lightly for 15 seconds. Transfer to a plate.

When ready to serve transfer the vegetables and sauce to a shallow bowl. Sprinkle the almond and coriander mixture on top and serve.

Note: for a hotter flavour add 1 teaspoon chilli powder to the sauce with the paprika.

CURRIED AUBERGINE WITH CHUTNEY

BAIGAN BHONA

An Anglo-Indian favourite, this curry-flavoured aubergine is savoury and delicious, a perfect vegetable to serve with *tandoori* meats (see Chapter 5) or simple grilled or roast beef, lamb or chicken. I also like to sandwich it between two slices of bread with lettuce and tomato for a satisfying vegetarian snack.

SERVES 4

1 large aubergine (about 1¼ lb/625 g)

1 medium onion, peeled and cut into ¼ in/5 mm slices

2 teaspoons curry powder

¼ teaspoon ground ginger

6 tablespoons vegetable oil

½ teaspoon salt

2 teaspoons lemon juice

2 tablespoons chutney (see Note below)

Cut the aubergine in half lengthways. Cut each half lengthways into 4 slices. Cut each slice into 1 in/2.5 cm wide pieces and put into a bowl. Add the onion, curry powder and ginger. Toss to mix.

Heat the oil in a large frying pan over high heat. Add the aubergine and sauté, tossing frequently, for 3 minutes. Reduce the heat and cook, tossing, uncovered, until the aubergine is tender (25 minutes). Turn off the heat, stir in the salt, lemon juice and chutney, and serve hot or at room temperature.

Note: you may use any chutney in this recipe from the Chutneys and Relishes (see Chapter 9). Particularly good choices are Tomato and Plum Chutney, Royal Peach Chutney, and Tamarind and Ginger Chutney. Commercially available mango chutney would also be excellent.

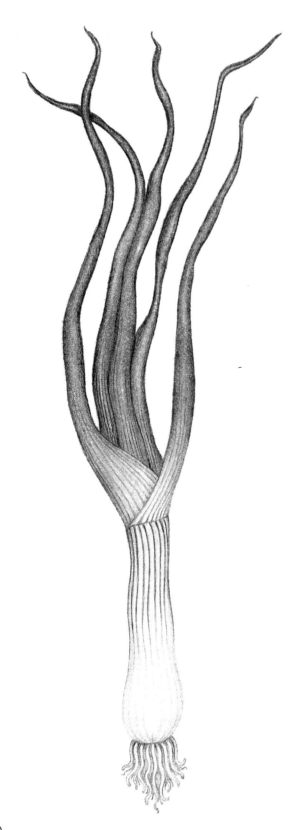

CAULIFLOWER WITH GINGER

GOBHI SABZI

Of all the vegetables, Indians like cauliflower the most. In this recipe, it is lightly spiced and combined with fresh ginger, then fried to give the dish a delicate herbal fragrance and retain the natural aroma of the cauliflower. It can be served with all the spicy stews (see Chapter 6).

SERVES 6

1 medium cauliflower (about 1½ lb/750 g)	*½ teaspoon turmeric*
3 tablespoons vegetable oil	*1 tablespoon shredded fresh ginger*
1½ teaspoons ground cumin	*1 teaspoon salt*
	4 fl oz/125 ml hot water
1 tablespoon ground coriander	*2 spring onions, trimmed and chopped*

Separate the cauliflower into very small florets, cutting them with a knife if necessary. Wash them in running cold water and drain.

Heat the oil over high heat in a large frying pan. When the oil is hot add the cauliflower. Sprinkle with the cumin, coriander, turmeric, ginger and salt. Sauté, turning and tossing the vegetables until the cauliflower is evenly coated with the spices (3 minutes).

Add the hot water, reduce the heat and cook, covered, until the cauliflower is fully cooked but still firm (about 10-12 minutes). Uncover, increase the heat and stir-fry until excess moisture has evaporated and the cauliflower looks glazed. Sprinkle with the chopped spring onions and serve.

VARIATION

For a hotter dish stir in 2 chopped green chillies and/or ¼ teaspoon chilli powder along with the other spices while cooking the cauliflower.

COURGETTES WITH MUSTARD FLAVOURING

LAU BHOJIA

A light and fragrant side dish or first course. It can be used as a filling for omelettes, too.

SERVES 4

2 tablespoons vegetable oil

1 teaspoon cumin seeds

1 tablespoon shredded fresh ginger

4 green chillies, sliced

1 lb/500 g courgettes, cut into strips, about 3 in/7 cm long and ¼ in/ 5 mm thick

1 medium ripe tomato, peeled, seeded and shredded

2 teaspoons lemon juice

2 teaspoons prepared mustard

2 tablespoons finely chopped coriander leaves

1 teaspoon salt

For the garnish

chopped coriander leaves (optional)

Heat the oil in a large frying pan over high heat for 3 minutes. Add the cumin, let it turn a few shades darker (about 20 seconds), then add the ginger and chillies. Cook for 30 seconds more. Add the courgettes and fry, turning and tossing, for 10 minutes. Add the tomato during the last 3 minutes of cooking.

Stir in the lemon juice, mustard, coriander and salt and continue cooking for another 2 minutes or until the vegetables are cooked but still crisp and evenly coated with the seasonings.

Transfer the vegetables to a warm serving platter and, if desired, garnish with the coriander.

Note: this dish may be prepared ahead and kept at room temperature for a couple of hours. Heat thoroughly before serving.

MADRAS MUSHROOMS WITH CURRY

KHUMBI KARI

These curry-scented mushrooms are good with drinks, as a first course, or at breakfast with fried sausage and eggs.

SERVES 4

3 tablespoons sesame or vegetable oil

1 lb/500 g mushrooms, cut into 1 in/2.5 cm pieces

4 oz/125 g chopped onion

1 teaspoon finely chopped garlic

2 teaspoons curry powder

1 teaspoon salt, or to taste

1 tablespoon lemon juice

2 tablespoons chopped coriander leaves

Heat the oil in a large frying pan over moderately high heat. When the oil is hot, add the mushrooms and cook, turning and tossing, until lightly browned and beginning to steam (5 minutes). Add the onion, garlic, curry powder and salt. Continue cooking until excess moisture released by the mushrooms has evaporated and the mushrooms look fried (about 10 minutes). Sprinkle with the lemon juice and coriander and serve hot, at room temperature, or cold.

Note: this dish can be prepared ahead and kept refrigerated for up to 2 days. If so it may be served as is, chilled or heated through.

CREAMED LENTILS WITH FRAGRANT SPICE BUTTER

DAL

A golden purée of lentils laced with spices and herbs, *dal* is served with all traditional Indian meals.

SERVES 4

8 oz/250 g lentils	1 teaspoon cumin seeds
1¼ pt/750 ml water, more as needed	½ teaspoon mustard seeds
½ teaspoon turmeric	2 bay leaves
1 teaspoon salt	4 large cloves garlic, peeled and sliced thickly
For the spiced butter or oil	½ teaspoon paprika (or chilli powder for a hotter flavour)
3 tablespoons usli ghee, concentrated butter or vegetable oil	

Put the lentils, water, turmeric and salt in a large pan. Bring to the boil. Reduce the heat, cover partially and boil gently, until cooked and tender (30-40 minutes). Stir a few times during cooking to ensure the lentils are not sticking to the pan and burning. Add more water if necessary. Turn off the heat and check the consistency. It should be like a thin cream soup, if not, add more water. Cover the pan.

Heat the *usli ghee*, butter or oil in a frying pan. When the *ghee* is hot, add the cumin and mustard. When the mustard seeds begin to splutter add the bay leaves. If they splutter too much cover the pan briefly with a lid. When the mustard seeds stop spluttering add the garlic and fry until it turns golden. Turn off the heat. Add the paprika or chilli powder, shake the pan for a second or two and immediately pour the contents over the lentils. Stir just a few times to streak the lentils with the spice-laced butter. Serve immediately.

VARIATION

Replace the lentils with yellow split peas.

Note: this dish can be made ahead and refrigerated for up to 2 days. Reheat thoroughly to serve.

Dal may also be served by itself as a soup course, if you wish.

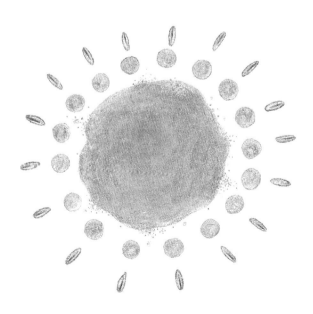

CHICK-PEAS IN TOMATO AND GINGER SAUCE

CHANA MASALA

These spicy, tart chick-peas in a gingery tomato sauce are ideal served at brunch or lunch accompanied by *Poori* (p. 30) and Spicy Lemon Chutney (p. 82).

SERVES 4

3 tablespoons
vegetable oil

1 medium onion,
sliced thinly

1 teaspoon finely
chopped garlic

½ teaspoon lovage
seeds or 1 teaspoon
dried thyme

2 teaspoons ground
cumin

1 teaspoon
mustard powder

2 tablespoons chopped
fresh ginger

2 large tomatoes,
chopped into
large chunks,
with the skins on

1 lb/500 g canned
chick-peas with juices,
or 8 oz/225 g chick-
peas, soaked and cooked
with 4 fl oz/125 ml
cooking liquid

For the garnish

4 tablespoons finely
chopped coriander
leaves

2 green chillies,
sliced thinly
crossways

Heat the oil in a large pan over moderately high heat. Add the onion and garlic and fry until they turn light brown (about 5 minutes), stirring constantly to prevent burning. Stir in the lovage, cumin and mustard, and fry for 1 more minute.

Add the ginger and tomatoes, then the chick-peas and their liquid, mix well and bring to the boil. Lower the heat and cook, covered, for 15 minutes. Check the seasonings and add salt if necessary. Serve garnished with the coriander and chillies.

VARIATION

Substitute an equal quantity of red kidney beans, borlotti beans or haricot beans for the chick-peas.

Note: this dish may be made ahead and refrigerated for up to 4 days or frozen. Defrost thoroughly before heating. Check the seasonings, and if necessary, add a little (1 teaspoon) garam masala to perk up flavours.

8
SALADS

MINT-SCENTED ROASTED PEPPER AND YOGURT SALAD

MIRCH KA RAITA

This wonderful *raita*, filled with the delicate smoky aroma of roasted peppers, can be served with any main dish. It is good enough to be served by itself accompanied by a stuffed Indian bread.

SERVES 4

1 medium green pepper, roasted (see below) and cut into ¼ in/5 mm cubes	*15 oz/450 g thick set natural yogurt*
1 medium red pepper, roasted (see below) and cut into ¼ in/5 mm cubes	*2 tablespoons finely chopped mint leaves*
1 medium cucumber, peeled and grated	*2 tablespoons finely chopped onion*
	½ teaspoon salt

Put all the ingredients in a bowl, mix thoroughly and chill before serving.

Roasted Pepper

To roast a pepper, place it over the highest flame of a gas burner and roast, turning the pepper until it is well charred on all sides (about 10 minutes). Transfer the pepper to a small paper bag and fold it shut to let the pepper sweat, thus making its skin loose. Alternatively, place the pepper, cut in half with its skin side up, under a preheated electric grill until charred; then bag as above.

When the pepper is slightly cool rub the skin off with your fingers. Deseed as usual.

VARIATIONS

To transform the salad into a very refreshing dip for fried foods, purée the entire salad, in batches, in a food processor or an electric blender. Add 8 fl oz/250 ml (or more as necessary) buttermilk and blend it in. To turn the salad into a hearty luncheon dish, fold in 12 oz/375 g cooked sliced chicken meat, ½ teaspoon prepared mustard and 2 tablespoons finely chopped mango chutney.

Note: this yogurt salad may be made ahead and refrigerated for up to a day. Refrigerate the vegetables separately and fold them into the yogurt just before serving.

CARROT AND YOGURT SALAD WITH RAISINS AND WALNUTS

KASHMIRI RAITA

In Kashmir, this wonderful nutmeg-laced salad is made with freshly picked green walnuts. For best results use sweet juicy carrots.

SERVES 4

1 lb/500 g carrots, peeled and grated	⅛ teaspoon freshly grated nutmeg or ¼ teaspoon ground cardamom
6 oz/175 g thick set natural yogurt	
2 tablespoons honey or jaggery syrup (or use liquid cane syrup)	½ teaspoon salt
	2 oz/50 g dark raisins
	2 oz/50 g chopped walnuts

Bring 3 pt/1.8 litres water to the boil in a pan. Add the carrots and cook for 1 minute. Drain immediately, rinse with cold water and drain again. Arrange the carrot shreds in a shallow serving dish.

Mix the yogurt, honey, nutmeg and salt thoroughly in a bowl and pour over the carrots. Arrange the raisins and walnuts on top. Fold the salad gently and serve.

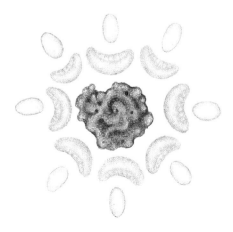

MIXED VEGETABLE SALAD IN YOGURT DRESSING

SABZI RAITA

Flavoured in the classic northern style, this *raita* is an ideal accompaniment to all Moghul dishes, northern curries and *tandoori* meats.

SERVES 4

15 oz/450 g thick set natural yogurt	1½ teaspoons ground roasted cumin seeds
1½ lb/750 g cooked mixed vegetables (such as spinach, carrots, courgettes, potatoes, green beans, green peas, broad beans and cabbage), cut into ½ in/1 cm cubes	2 tablespoons finely chopped coriander leaves
	¼ teaspoon black pepper
½ teaspoon salt, or to taste	¼ teaspoon paprika (or chilli powder for a hotter flavour)

Combine the yogurt, vegetables, salt and cumin in a bowl until thoroughly blended. Transfer to a shallow serving dish, sprinkle with the coriander, black pepper and paprika, and serve.

VARIATIONS

Spinach and Yogurt Salad
Use 1½ lb/750 g cooked, chopped spinach and add 1½ teaspoons ground roasted coriander seeds when the salad is mixed in place of the garnish of coriander leaves.

Mixed Nuts and Dried Fruit Salad
Substitute 4 oz/125 g chopped mixed nuts (such as walnuts, almonds, cashew nuts, pistachios), 4 oz/125 g dried fruit (such as apples, figs, peaches, apricots, dates, prunes) and 1 medium cucumber, peeled and grated, for the vegetables.

Note: this yogurt salad may be made ahead and refrigerated for up to 2 days.

MANGO AND YOGURT SALAD

MANGA PACHADI

A cooling contrast to spicy food.

SERVES 4

15 oz/450 g thick set natural yogurt	1 tablespoon sesame or vegetable oil
½ teaspoon salt	1 teaspoon mustard seeds
1 medium, ripe mango, peeled, stoned, and flesh cut into ½ in/1 cm cubes	2 tablespoons roasted cashew nuts (p. 26) chopped coarsely
1 tablespoon white sugar	pinch of freshly grated nutmeg

Put the yogurt and salt in a bowl, and stir to mix. Add the mango and sugar and carefully fold them into the yogurt.

Heat the oil in a small frying pan over high heat. When the oil is hot add the mustard seeds. Keep a lid handy since the seeds may splutter. When the seeds stop spluttering and turn grey, turn off the heat. Immediately pour the entire contents of the pan over the yogurt and mango mixture. Stir carefully, just enough to mix.

Transfer to a serving dish and garnish with the cashew nuts. Sprinkle with a little nutmeg and serve.

VARIATION

Substitute an equal amount of any other fruit for the mangoes. Particularly good choices are pineapple, banana, apples, peaches, papaya and oranges.

Note: this yogurt salad may be made ahead and kept refrigerated for up to 3 days.

POTATO AND SHALLOT SALAD

PODIMAS

This is a classic south Indian Brahmin salad generally served for lunch and on picnics. For variety fold in 2 oz/50 g cooked green peas.

SERVES 4

1 lb/500 g potatoes, boiled, peeled and cut into 1 in/2.5 cm cubes	1 teaspoon mustard seeds
2 green chillies, chopped finely	3 oz/75 g shallots, chopped finely
1½ teaspoons curry powder	1 tablespoon lemon juice
1¼ teaspoons salt	2 tablespoons finely chopped coriander leaves
3 tablespoons vegetable oil	

Combine potatoes, chillies, curry powder and salt in a bowl. Heat the oil in a large frying pan over high heat. When the oil is hot add mustard seeks. Keep a lid handy since the seeds may splutter. When the seeds stop spluttering and turn grey, reduce the heat, add the shallots and cook for 2 minutes, then add the potato mixture. Stir-fry until the potatoes are lightly browned and look glazed (10 minutes). Turn off the heat, stir in lemon juice and half of the coriander leaves and serve garnished with the remainder.

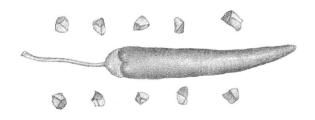

9

CHUTNEYS AND RELISHES

COCONUT CHUTNEY

NARIAL CHATNI

Here is a chutney for coconut lovers – filled with the delicate sweetness of coconut and spices. It goes well with all fish, seafood and poultry dishes.

MAKES ABOUT ½ pt/300 ml

8 oz/250 g fresh grated coconut, desiccated coconut or a block of coconut cream

1 in/2.5 cm cube fresh ginger, peeled

2 green chillies, chopped coarsely

4 oz/125 g natural yogurt

2 teaspoons white sugar

½ teaspoon salt

1 tablespoon vegetable oil

1 teaspoon mustard seeds

Put the coconut, ginger, chillies, yogurt, sugar and salt into the container of an electric blender or food processor. Run the machine until the ingredients are finely puréed and the chutney looks like a thick pulpy sauce. Transfer to a bowl.

Heat the oil in a small frying pan until very hot. Add the mustard seeds. Keep a lid handy as the seeds may splutter and fly about. When the seeds stop spluttering, pour the contents of the pan over the coconut mixture. Mix well and serve.

VARIATIONS

Coriander and Coconut Chutney
Add 2 tablespoons finely chopped coriander leaves with the coconut.

Tomato and Coconut Chutney
Add 4 oz/125 g fresh ripe tomatoes, peeled and seeded, with the coconut.

Onion and Coconut Chutney
Add 4 tablespoons chopped onion to the hot oil after the mustard seeds stop spluttering, and fry until they are soft and glazed. Fold the entire contents into the coconut mixture, mix and serve.

Note: the chutney may be made ahead and refrigerated for up to 5 days, or frozen. Defrost thoroughly and stir well to mix before serving.

Mint Chutney

POODINA CHATNI

Very fragrant and slightly hot, this mint chutney is perfect served with fried food, roast and grilled meats, and of course, *tandoori* meats.

MAKES ABOUT ½ pt/300 ml

7 fl oz/200 ml white wine vinegar

1 in/2.5 cm cube fresh ginger, peeled

2 oz/50 g chopped unripe green mango pulp, or 1 small green pepper, cored and chopped

1 teaspoon salt

6 green chillies, chopped coarsely

1 teaspoon salt

1½ oz/40 g white sugar

4 oz/125 g mint leaves, chopped coarsely

4 oz/125 g coriander leaves, including the stalks, if tender, chopped coarsely

Put all the ingredients into the container of an electric blender or food processor. Run the machine, turning it off often and pushing the herbs down with a rubber spatula, until the contents are reduced to a sauce. Transfer to a small bowl and serve.

VARIATION

For a sweetish-sour flavour stir 4 fl oz/125 ml apricot purée or 2 fl oz/50 ml tamarind pulp into the chutney.

Note: the mint chutney may be prepared ahead and kept at room temperature for up to 8 hours, or 4 days in the refrigerator, or frozen. Defrost thoroughly and stir to mix well before serving.

North Indian Vegetable Relish

KACHOOMAR

An ideal accompaniment for *tandoori* meats, roasts and grilled chicken, lamb or beef.

SERVES 4

1 medium green pepper, cored and chopped into ¼ in/5 mm pieces

1 medium tomato, chopped into ¼ in/5 mm pieces

1 medium onion, peeled and chopped into ¼ in/5 mm pieces

2 oz/50 g coriander leaves, chopped

1 tablespoon lemon juice

½ teaspoon salt, or to taste

1 green chilli, minced (optional)

Put all the ingredients in a bowl, toss well to mix and serve.

Note: this relish can be prepared ahead and refrigerated for up to a day. For best results add the salt just before serving.

TAMARIND AND GINGER CHUTNEY

SOONTH

A very popular sweet and spicy dipping sauce for fritters, kebabs and other fried food.

MAKES ABOUT 2¼ pt/1.3 litres

8 oz/250 g tamarind paste	½ teaspoon black pepper
3½ pt/2 litres water	½ teaspoon cardamom
3 oz/75 g white sugar	2 teaspoons ground cumin or garam masala
1 teaspoon salt	
2 teaspoons paprika	1 tablespoon ground ginger
4 or more green chillies, minced	4 tablespoons shredded fresh ginger

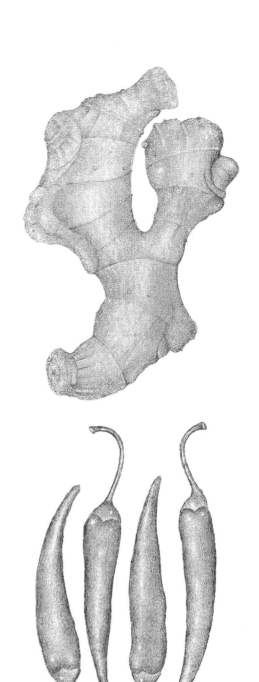

Break the tamarind into small pieces by pulling it apart. Put it in an enamelled pan. Add 2¼ pt/1.5 litres of the water and bring to the boil. Cook, uncovered, over moderate heat, at a gentle boil for 30 minutes. Add the remaining water and continue cooking for an additional 30 minutes.

Turn off the heat. When cool, mash the tamarind with a wooden or plastic spoon to extract as much pulp as possible and dissolve it in water. Strain the liquid, mashing the pulp, into a bowl. Rinse the pan and return the tamarind liquid to it.

Add all the other ingredients and bring to the boil. Cook, over moderate heat, simmering until the spices lose their raw smell and flavour (about 10 minutes). Turn off the heat. Cool thoroughly (and preferably chill) before serving. The chutney has the consistency of a thin dipping sauce.

Note: the chutney may be made ahead and kept at room temperature for up to 8 hours, or for 2 weeks in the refrigerator, or frozen. Defrost thoroughly and stir well to mix the ingredients before serving.

SPICY LEMON CHUTNEY

TOKKOO

A very hot and spicy spread. This is a perfect accompaniment to Moghul dishes that are mild and need an additional punch.

MAKES ABOUT 1 pt/600 ml

8 lemons, quartered

2 tablespoons chilli powder

1/2 tablespoon turmeric

2 teaspoons ground cumin

2 teaspoons mustard powder

2 tablespoons salt

4 fl oz/125 ml sesame, groundnut or vegetable oil

2 tablespoons finely chopped shallots or red onion

Put the lemons into the container of a food processor and run the machine until they are finely minced or, alternatively, chop the lemons extremely finely with a knife.

Transfer to a non-metallic bowl, stir in the chilli powder, turmeric, cumin, mustard and salt, and set aside.

Heat the oil in a medium enamelled pan. When the oil is hot, add the shallots or onion and cook, stirring, until it looks soft and begins to brown (2 minutes).

Add the lemon mixture. Lower the heat and cook the mixture, stirring, until the contents of the pan reduce to a thick pulp and the oil begins to separate (about 10 minutes). If necessary regulate the heat between moderate and moderately high.

Pour the chutney into sterilized jar(s) and seal.

Note: this chutney is ready to use immediately. Store in the refrigerator for up to 6 months.

TOMATO AND PLUM CHUTNEY

TAMATAR-ALOO BOKHARA CHATNI

This chutney goes extremely well with both Indian and Western menus.

MAKES ABOUT 2 pt/1.2 litres

8 fl oz/250 ml white wine vinegar

2 oz/50 g fresh ginger

8 large garlic cloves

9 oz/275 g white sugar

2 lb/1 kg ripe red tomatoes, peeled, seeded and cut into 1 in/2.5 cm wedges

2 lb/1 kg red plums, stoned and cut into 1 in/2.5 cm wedges

2 teaspoons ground ginger

1 teaspoon mustard powder

1/4 teaspoon ground cloves

2 teaspoons salt

1 teaspoon chilli powder

2 teaspoons paprika

juice of 1 large lemon

Put 4 fl oz/125 ml of the vinegar into the container of an electric blender or a food processor. Add the fresh ginger and garlic and run the machine until finely puréed. Pour the purée into a large enamelled pan, add the remaining vinegar and the sugar and bring to the boil. Cook the mixture until it is slightly thick and syrupy (6-8 minutes).

Add the tomatoes, plums and all the other ingredients. Stir well and bring to the boil again. Lower the heat and boil the chutney gently until it is thick and pulpy (40 minutes). Pour the chutney into sterilized jars and seal. The chutney is ready to use immediately. It will keep for 6 months in a cool place.

VARIATION

Stir in 2 oz/50 g chopped walnuts, sliced almonds or pine nuts, and 2 oz/50 g sultanas with the tomatoes and plums.

ROYAL PEACH CHUTNEY

SHAHI CHATNI

A royal chutney indeed – flavoured with saffron, this delicate chutney may be reserved for important occasions. It goes well with all Moghul dishes, Anglo-Indian dishes, and roasts.

MAKES ABOUT 2 pt/1.2 litres

2 lb/1 kg firm ripe peaches

½ pt/300 ml white wine vinegar

8 oz/250 g sugar

½ teaspoon ground cinnamon

1½ teaspoons mustard powder

½ teaspoon chilli powder

¼ teaspoon ground cloves

1 teaspoon ground ginger

1 teaspoon salt

2 tablespoons raisins

½ teaspoon saffron threads

4 tablespoons roasted sliced almonds

juice of 1 lemon

½ teaspoon shredded lemon zest

Peel and stone the peaches and cut the fruit into 1 in/2.5 cm pieces.

Put the fruit in a large enamelled pan along with 8 fl oz/250 ml of the vinegar, and bring to the boil. Cook the fruit until it is barely tender but cooked through (about 7 minutes). Turn off the heat and let the fruit sit in the liquid for 5 minutes. Transfer the fruit to a bowl with a slotted spoon, reserving the liquid.

To the same pan add the remaining vinegar and the sugar and bring it to the boil again. Boil the syrup gently until it turns sticky (about 15 minutes).

Add the cinnamon, mustard, chilli powder, cloves, ginger, salt, raisins and saffron along with the reserved fruit. Continue cooking over moderate heat until the contents of the pan look thick and glazed like a jam (about 10 minutes).

Turn off the heat, and stir in the almonds, lemon juice and zest. Pour the chutney into sterilized jars and seal.

VARIATION

Substitute an equal amount of fresh nectarines, apricots, plums or pineapple (or a combination) for the peaches.

Note: the chutney is ready to use immediately. It keeps well for 6 months. Store opened jars in the refrigerator.

10
DESSERTS, SWEETMEATS & DRINKS

QUICK YOGURT PUDDING

SRIKHAND

Here is a delicate pudding made with yogurt, soured cream and cream cheese, lightly sweetened and then laced with the scent of saffron and nutmeg. You must try this to believe how good yogurt can taste!

SERVES 4

8 oz/250 g natural yogurt	¼ teaspoon saffron threads, crushed lightly
5 tablespoons soured cream	¼ teaspoon freshly grated nutmeg
4 oz/125 g cream cheese	**For the garnish**
1 oz/25 g icing sugar	1 tablespoon unsalted pistachios, sliced

Combine all the ingredients in a bowl, mix thoroughly and spoon into individual dessert bowls or stemmed glasses. Sprinkle with the sliced pistachios, chill and serve.

VARIATIONS

This is the basic yogurt pudding recipe. With the addition of fruits and nuts it can be expanded into more complex desserts. Fruits such as mangoes, pineapple, peaches, bananas, grapes, cherries, papayas, or nectarines, and all varieties of berries, are suitable. Nuts such as almonds, cashew nuts, and pine nuts are particularly good.

The pudding can be transformed into a sensational dessert sauce by stirring in 8 fl oz/250 ml single cream or milk and 4 fl oz/125 ml fruit liqueur or fruit juice (passion fruit, apricot, peach or orange). Serve the sauce with pancakes, apple fritters or simply with sliced fresh fruits such as mangoes, papayas, kiwi, oranges, strawberries, peaches and pears. Sprinkle the nuts for garnish over the fruits and dust the sauce with a little nutmeg.

To transform the pudding into a frozen dessert, increase sugar to 2 oz/50 g and mix the nuts for garnish into the pudding and freeze the mixture in

an ice-cream freezer following manufacturer's instructions.

Note: the pudding may be made ahead and refrigerated for up to 5 days or frozen. Defrost thoroughly and stir well before serving.

BURFI OF NUTS

BURFI

This is the Indian equivalent of the Middle-Eastern *halva* or the French *petits fours*.

MAKES ABOUT 36 BURFI

3 oz/75 g unsalted butter

8 oz/250 g blanched almonds and cashew nuts, mixed

1 pt/600 ml milk, scalded

6 oz/175 g sugar, white or light brown

½ teaspoon ground cardamom or ¼ teaspoon orange flower water

⅓ teaspoon screwpine essence (optional)

For the garnish

slivered almonds

2-4 pieces silver leaf (optional)

Melt 1 oz/25 g of the butter in a heavy-bottomed pan over moderately high heat. Add the nuts and stir until they begin to brown. Reduce the heat and cook, stirring constantly, until the nuts turn a light golden brown (about 5 minutes). Drain them on kitchen paper and transfer to a medium bowl. Add the hot milk, cover and let soak for 2 hours.

Purée the nut and milk mixture in a blender until smooth and thick. Pour into the original pan. Cook the mixture over moderately high heat until most of the milk has evaporated and the paste mounds in a spoon (10 minutes). Reduce the heat and add the sugar, remaining butter and cardamom. Cook, stirring, until the contents develop the consistency of fudge (10-12 minutes).

Stir in the screwpine essence, and pour the mixture into a 9 in/23 cm square baking dish. Cool slightly then pat into an even layer. Cut the fudge into 1 in/2.5 cm squares or diamonds. Store in airtight containers. Serve garnished with slivered almonds and silver leaf if liked (see below).

Garnishing with silver leaf: if you are using silver leaf, peel off one paper. Pick up the silver leaf with the other paper still attached and gently drop the silver leaf on the fudge before cutting it. Press gently.

Note: this *burfi* keeps well at room temperature for 2 weeks or in the refrigerator for 2 months, or it can be frozen.

Banana and Rice Pudding with Raisins and Almonds

KELE KA KHEER

Rice pudding, the comfort food of millions, has many interpretations around the world. Here is a popular version from northern India made with bananas. You can substitute mango, peaches, apricots, passion fruit or pumpkin in place of the banana.

SERVES 6

2½ pt/1.5 litres milk

2 tablespoons blanched almonds

5 tablespoons long grain rice

1 large banana, peeled and mashed

3 tablespoons honey or brown sugar

½ teaspoon ground cardamom

¼ teaspoon saffron threads

4 tablespoons dark raisins

For the garnish

sliced almonds (optional)

Bring ½ pt/300 ml of milk to the boil in a large pan. Add the almonds and turn off the heat. Let the almonds soak for 15 minutes.

Pour the milk with the almonds into the container of an electric blender. Process until the contents are thoroughly puréed. Return the mixture to the pan, add the remaining milk and rice and bring to the boil again. Simmer the milk over medium-low heat, so that it bubbles gently until the rice is very tender and the pudding thickens (about 1 hour). Stir frequently while it is cooking.

Stir in the banana, honey or sugar, cardamom, saffron and raisins. Cook for an additional 10 minutes or until the pudding thickens to the consistency of tapioca pudding. Cool and refrigerate to chill. To serve, spoon the pudding into goblets and sprinkle with sliced almonds, if you wish.

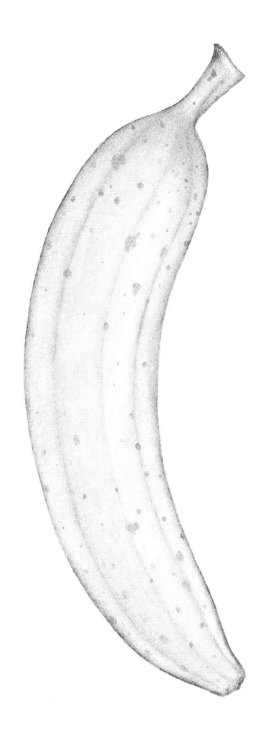

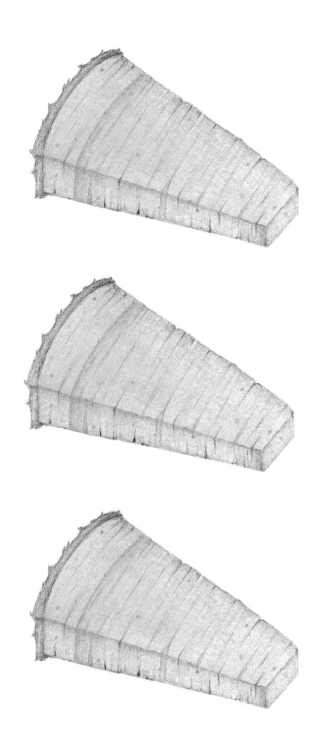

MANGO FOOL

MANGOPHUL

An all-time favourite of the Anglo-Indians, Mango Fool is the lightest pudding imaginable.

SERVES 8

½ pt/300 ml
single cream

4 tablespoons sugar

2 tablespoons cornflour,
dissolved in 4
tablespoons single cream
or milk

¾ pt/450 ml puréed
fresh mango pulp or
canned mango purée

½ teaspoon almond
essence

1 tablespoon
lemon juice

4 tablespoons liqueur
(combination of cognac
and orange liqueur)

½ pt/300 ml
double cream,
whipped until stiff

24 thin slices of fresh
pineapple or mango

For the garnish

mint sprigs (optional)

Heat the single cream and sugar in a small pan over moderate heat. When the cream comes to the boil, stir in the cornflour mixture. Cook until the cream thickens and forms a custard (about 2 minutes). Let it cool thoroughly.

Put the custard with the mango pulp, almond essence, lemon juice and liqueur into the container of an electric blender or food processor. Run the machine until the contents are thoroughly blended and develop a smooth texture.

Transfer the custard to a bowl, fold in the whipped cream and chill thoroughly. Spoon the dessert on to 8 individual dessert plates. Arrange 3 slices of pineapple or mango in a fan on each. Serve, if desired, garnished with a sprig of mint.

Note: Mango Fool may be made ahead and refrigerated for up to 5 days.

INDIAN MANGO ICE-CREAM

KULFI, AAM

This is the Indian version of ice-cream. It is made by cooking the milk down to a single cream consistency, and sweetening and flavouring it with mangoes and nutmeg before freezing it. It has a palate-teasing texture, something between ice-cream and sorbet.

SERVES 6

1½ pt/900 ml milk	5 tablespoons honey
½ pt/300 ml double cream	8 fl oz/250 ml puréed fresh mango pulp or 6 fl oz/175 ml canned mango purée
¼ teaspoon grated nutmeg	

Combine the milk and cream in a medium heavy-bottomed pan and bring to the boil. Reduce the heat and cook the milk, gently bubbling, stirring often, until it reduces to 1¼ pt/750 ml (about 35-45 minutes). Set aside to cool.

When cool, stir in the nutmeg, honey and mango pulp. Pour the mixture into 6 *kulfi* moulds, distributing it evenly, or use deep bun tins lined with clingfilm. Cover with foil and freeze until set (about 4 hours).

To serve, remove the *kulfis* by running a sharp knife around the inside surface of each mould. If necessary dip the moulds in hot water to loosen them. Slip each one on to a serving plate and cut crossways into 3-4 slices and serve.

VARIATIONS

Substitute any other fruit pulp for the mango pulp to make different fruit *kulfis*.

To make saffron *kulfi*, omit the mango pulp in the recipe and substitute ½ teaspoon saffron threads, lightly powdered.

Note: kulfi can be made ahead and kept in the freezer for up to 2 months.

LOW-CALORIE YOGURT DRINK

LASSI

A very nutritious and tasty drink made with low-fat yogurt, *lassi* is great with meals on hot summer afternoons, at the beach and on picnics.

SERVES 2

1¼ lb/600 g natural low fat yogurt	½ teaspoon rose essence or orange flower water
1½ tablespoons honey	8 ice cubes
½ teaspoon salt	

Put the yogurt, honey, salt and essence into the container of an electric blender and run the machine for 30 seconds or until the ingredients are blended. Add the ice cubes and continue blending for another 30 seconds or until the yogurt drink is frothy (the ice cubes will not disintegrate fully). Pour the drink, with the ice cubes, into tall glasses and serve.

VARIATION

For a savoury *lassi*, replace the honey and essence with 1 tablespoon fresh mint leaves and ¼ teaspoon ground cumin.

Note: lassi can be made ahead and kept refrigerated for up to 3 days. Froth the *lassi* in the electric blender before serving.

LOW-CALORIE BUTTERMILK AND FRUIT DRINK

AAM LASSI

A light and refreshing drink made with fully ripe fragrant mangoes and buttermilk. I reach for this whenever I get a craving for sweets!

SERVES 2

8 fl oz/250 ml fresh mango purée or canned puréed mango

¾ pt/450 ml buttermilk

1 teaspoon lemon juice

½ teaspoon salt

1 tablespoon honey

pinch of nutmeg

8 ice cubes

Put the mango purée, buttermilk, lemon juice, salt, honey and nutmeg into the container of an electric blender. Run the machine until the ingredients are blended (30 seconds). Add the ice cubes and continue blending for another 30 seconds or until the drink is frothy (the ice cubes will not disintegrate fully). Pour the drink, with the ice cubes, into tall glasses and serve.

VARIATION

To make different fruit-flavoured drinks, substitute an equal amount of fruit such as papayas, peaches, apricots, bananas, strawberries, blueberries or raspberries (or any combination) for the mango.

90

GINGER LIMEADE

SHIKANJI

A refreshing twist to standard lemonade or limeade – this Indian version uses fresh ginger with fabulous results.

SERVES 4

4 fl oz/125 ml freshly squeezed lime juice

1½ teaspoons fresh ginger juice (see below)

8 oz/250 g white sugar

1 pt/600 ml water

For the garnish

4 slices lime

4 thin slices fresh ginger

Combine the lime juice and ginger juice in a small non-metallic bowl and set aside.

Put the sugar and water in a small pan and bring to the boil over low heat, stirring often. Let the syrup boil for 30 seconds. Remove from the heat.

When the syrup is cool stir in the lime and ginger mixture. Chill thoroughly. To serve, pour the limeade evenly into tall glasses filled half-way with ice-cold water. Add enough ice cubes to fill the glass to the top. Stir carefully and serve.

Note: to extract ginger juice press peeled and chopped fresh ginger through a garlic press.

SPICED CITRUS TEA

CHAH DIL-BAHAAR

This herbal infusion is very refreshing served either hot or chilled over ice. A very fragrant tea to end a spicy Indian meal.

SERVES 8

1¼ pt/750 ml cold water	½ × 3 in/1 × 7 cm strip of orange peel
3 in/7.5 cm stick cinnamon	½ × 3 in/1 × 7 cm strip of grapefruit peel
4 whole cloves	6 teaspoons leaf tea or 6 teabags (orange pekoe)
¼ teaspoon fennel seeds	
½ × 3 in/1 × 7 cm strip of lemon peel	

Bring the water to the boil in a deep pan. Add the spices, blend and turn off the heat. Cover the pan and let spices soak for at least 10 minutes.

Add the peels to the pan and bring the water to the boil again. Add the tea and let it brew, covered, for 3 minutes. Strain the tea into a teapot and serve.

CLASSIC INDIAN TEA

PAHADI CHAH

This is the famous Indian tea, also known as Frontier Brew, that sustained the Gurkha regiment during World War Two. For a less potent version substitute water for part of the milk and reduce the sugar as desired.

SERVES 2

1 pt/600 ml milk	2 oz/50 g jaggery or 2 heaped teaspoons brown sugar
2 heaped teaspoons leaf tea or 3 teabags	

Combine milk, tea and jaggery in a small pan and bring to the boil. Simmer the tea, partially covered, for 5 minutes. Turn off the heat and let the tea brew for another minute then strain it into a teapot and serve.

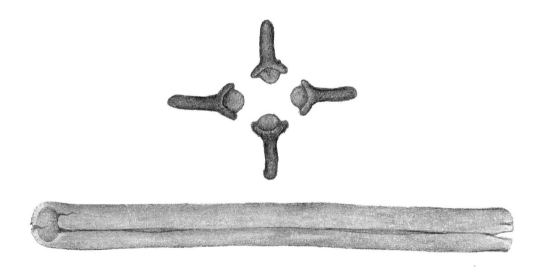

INDEX